An Overview of Consumers' Awareness towards Eco-Friendly Products

Dr.K. Vidhyakala

Published by

BONFRING®
Intellectual Integrity

An Overview of Consumers' Awareness towards Eco-Friendly Products

9 789392 537073 >

ISBN 978-93-92537-07-3

Author

Dr.K. Vidhyakala

Bonfring

309, 5th Street Extension, Gandhipuram,

Coimbatore-641 012.

Tamil Nadu, India.

E-mail: info@bonfring.org

Website: www.bonfring.org

Acknowledgement

I would like to thank respective people that had an influence on the development of this book. First, I would like thank to each one of them for their encouragement, cooperation and moral support.

I would extend our thanks to one and all helped me directly and indirectly for successful completion of this book. Importantly, I would like to thank my parents, friends and all my family members for helping me realize about sustainability of daily lives.

I have great pleasure in expressing my deep sense of gratitude to Dr.P. Santhi, Professor, Department of Commerce, Avinashilingam Institute for Home Science and Higher Education for Women, Coimbatore for her encouragement and constructive suggestions and good wishes for the development of this book.

My special thanks to Dr.Chi. Nanjappa, Head, Department of Business Administration, Valluvar College of Science and Management, Karur, for his advice and also support me towards the betterment of this book.

I take this opportunity to express my profound thanks to the whole lot of the following eminent personalities. Without their involvement, guidance and knowledge this research work would not have been possible.

Finally, I wish to thank the readers of this book. An Overview about the Consumer Purchase Responsibility of Eco-Friendly to be a comprehensive approach to sustainably oriented practices.

Acknowledgement

TABLE OF CONTENTS

CHAPTER I

1. An Overview of Consumers' Awareness towards Eco-Friendly Products

1.1. Introduction

Environmental concerns have resulted in the rise of attention across the human society since last decade. Today, environmental awareness is spreading thick and fast and has directed the central and state governments to introduce programmes relevant to environmental issues at all levels and these programmes are pertaining to sustainable development. For several crucial aspects of the environment, society needs good indicators for sustainable development. The environmental concern on the consumption of eco-friendly products has become an increasingly important aspect of sustainable development. Thus the study will analyze the impact of environmental concern on the consumption of eco-friendly products.

The purchasers and users of the products from a firm are important stakeholders that influence the firm in many ways. Consumers influence the action of a firm when they elect to buy the organisation's product offerings or choose to purchase products from the competitors. Marketing strategies are intended to influence consumers' consumption towards a product and marketers use measures of consumers consumption to indicate the success of strategies. Consumer acquire many beliefs about products in their environment by myriad experiences. As many unnecessary, wasteful and harmful products and processes are part of everyday life, there is a need for awareness regarding eco-friendly products consumption of consumer.

The fields of business and marketing have shed some light on the determinants of environmental consciousness. In addition, some insights motivate the consumers to engage in green behavior and consumers may be willing to purchase the environmentally friendly products within certain constraints (Christopher Gan, 2008). Therefore, business success depends on the ability of marketing to make green alternatives (Grant 2007).

Factors underlying environmental behavior have been studied from different theoretical perspectives (Ebreo, 2002). Some aggregate measures are focused on the environmental outcomes of particular behaviours. (Lindasteg, 2009).

Decisions always require choice between different behaviours. Marketers are particularly interested in consumers purchase behavior. Behaviours are based on the intentions produced when consumers consciously choose from among alternative actions. Some voluntary behaviours of consumers habits and based on intentions. But, some behaviours are not voluntary and are affected largely by environmental factors. Environmental factors can affect consumer decision and to develop effective marketing strategies, marketers need to know the purchase decision of consumers.

Environmental Concern

Many consumers, have begun in recent years to incorporate environmental concerns in their personal buying decisions through the purchase and use of products and services perceived to be more environmentally friendly products.

Environmental Concern involves providing consumers with more eco-friendly and socially acceptable products, therefore green consumption must necessitate consuming products in a more sustainable and socially responsible way. The relationship between consumption of eco-friendly products and sustainable development has brought out an important association and have inter-connection with environmental concern.

Concerns related to the environment are evident in the increasingly environmentally conscious market place. The environmental concern which includes food safety, human health, environmental impact (Yiridoe et al., 2005) and availability of product information also support the intention to buy. Over the years, majority of the consumers have realized that their purchasing behaviour has a direct impact on many ecological problems (Laroche, 1996). People with environmental concern are expected to favour green product purchase which may likely vary with their socio-economic profile.

Eco-Friendly Products

The products manufactured through green technology that caused no environmental hazardous are called eco-friendly products (Monica loss, 2013). Green is one of the newest product classifications. A factor in considering the greenness of a product is that perception of environmental and social performance is influenced by situational factors related to the product use. The performance of green products relates to their impact on society and physical environment before, during and after consumption.

Consumers who buy green products are the most predominant in the green marketing strategy. A strong commitment to environmental sustainability in product design and manufacture can yield significant opportunities to grow the business. If the marketers want to sell a greener product to consumers, first one needs to understand the consumers about the issues and the determinants of consumer purchase decision towards green products.

To understand behavior of the consumers, the majority of studies measure behavioural indicators of ecologically conscious consumers (Zimmer, 1994) and other studies offered additional attitudinal or psychographic dimensions associated with green awareness and behavior (Stem, 1993).

The Influence of Environmental Concern on Consumer Behaviour investigated the variables that predict green buying and buying products that are environmentally beneficial. Mainieri et al. (1997). William Young et al. (2010), analyzed that incentives and labels would help consumers to concentrate their purchasing behaviour in green products. Effects of product attributes and demographic characteristics on consumer purchasing behaviour towards green products indicated that majority of the respondents purchased the green products (Christopher et al., 2008).

Consumers are willing to pay more to maintain a cleaner and greener environment and marketers also have the responsibility to make the consumers understand the need and benefits of green (Pavan Mishra and Payal Sharma, 2010). Healthy consumption life style is a good predictor for attitude toward organic food, meanwhile attitude toward organic food directly influence to buying intention toward organic food (Budi Suprapto and Tony Wijaya, 2012). The effect of green marketing on consumer's intention to purchase by considering the corporate image as an inter-mediatory in retail-sale environment indicated that green marketing has a significant effect on social responsibility and product image (Fariddeddin Allameh Haery et al, 2013).

Consumers' Awareness

Consumers' Awareness towards green foods consumption indicated that green food is not only about being organic but it also encompasses the concept of food safety, health issues, environmental hazard as well as animal welfare. Thus, most of the respondents were aware of the green concept which is a strong indicator of consumers' intention to go green in food consumption (Golnaz Rezai et al, 2012).

Consumers who have a higher monthly income and educational qualification are more likely to be concerned about the environment and therefore tend to purchase green products (Mahesh and Ganapathi, 2012). Socio demographic variables are not significantly related with green purchase intention. Besides this environmental advertisement, price and ecological packaging were found to be positively related with the green purchase intention (Novera Ansar, 2013). The role of customer's believability and attitude in green purchase intention measures the least damage to the environment (Mozhgan Irandust and Naser Bamdad, 2014).

Consumer Consumption

Consumption means using of resources in day to day life. Purchase done for household consumption are known as consumer consumption. There is a need to use consumption not just as an individual's choice among goods but as a stream of choices and decisions winding its way through the various stages of extraction, manufacture and final use. Purchasing behavior of individuals is unique because it involves different buying motives and it influences large variety of people.

Consumption of eco-friendly products is not a single activity but a serious of activities that can be inter-connected with environmental concern. Kardash, 1971 suggested that virtually green consumer can be classified as an ecologically concerned consumers. Sustainability involves development that meets the needs of the present without compromising the ability of future generations to meet their own needs.

1.2. Background of the Study

It is well-known fact that resources are limited and human wants are unlimited. Further environmental crises such as the global warming and depletion of ozone are to be taken care of for healthy survival. Worldwide evidence indicates that people are concerned about the environment and are changing their behavior. As a result, the awareness has increased among the consumers all over the world with regard to the protection of the environment. The marketing orientation is meant to focus a company on customer needs. An important challenge to be overcome is that different customers may purchase a particular product to fulfill different needs.

Eco-friendly products purchase lifestyles increase people's well-being (Jackson, 2005). Consumption of sustainable products is not a single activity, but a series of activities that can be interconnected with environmental concern. (Kardash, 1974) suggested that virtually green consumer can be classified as an ecologically concerned consumer. First and foremost, it is important to create a society which is sensitive and committed to the cause of environmental conservation enhancement. Successful environment – friendly initiatives have been carried out with an amalgamation of technology, aggregation and resource management for the youth of next generation.

Consumption represents consumers' usage of the acquired product. In general, purchase and consumption go hand in hand. Sometimes, purchases are made without knowing precisely when the consumption will occur. Different people may purchase the same product but consume it in different ways. (Roger D, 2018). The consumption of product is also influenced by the satisfaction attained by the consumer upon using the product.

1.3. Objectives

The objectives of the study are:

- To know the Awareness of consumers about the Eco-Friendly products.
- To study the environmental concern that influence the consumers on the Consumption of Eco-Friendly products and
- To identify the satisfaction of consumers on the consumption of Eco-Friendly products.

1.4. Statement of the Problem

In the present century, marketers need to understand the process by which consumers make their purchase and consumption decisions. The greater perceived importance is placed on consumer insight by awareness about the product and satisfaction through product consumption. The use of predictive exploration among the marketers is increasing these days. Predictive exploration generally emphasizes observing future purchase of consumers based on the frequency of purchasing a product. The frequency of purchase may be influenced by two factors namely satisfaction derived from consuming product or awareness about the product.

The impact of studying consumption of eco - friendly products brings academic understanding together with everyday life. Another great thing about studying consumption of eco-friendly products is that it exhibits possible solutions to environmental and social problems. Green marketing help individuals to make informed purchase decisions about green products purchase. In order to achieve a long-term sustainable development, the environmental impacts have to be reduced at industry level and individual household consumption level (Iris Gust, 2004). It predicts deliberate behaviour because behaviour can be deliberative or planned. Hence, an attempt is made to find out answer for the following questions:

- Are the consumers have the Awareness about the eco-friendly products?
- To what extent does the environmental concern impact the consumers on the purchase of eco-friendly products?
- Are the consumers satisfied on the consumption of Eco-Friendly products?

1.5. Interdisciplinary Relevance

The consumption of eco-friendly products is relevant to the aspect of environmental concern. Concerns connected with the environment are visible to the purchase of eco-friendly products. Hence, eco-friendly purchasing and consumption is facet in the change of lifestyle, sustainable development and human health.

1.6. Significance of the Study

In recent years due to rising evidence of environmental problems worldwide, the concern of the people about the environment has also increased. Previous empirical evidence emphasized that environmental concern is a major factor in the consumer decision making (Zimmer et al., 1994; Wagner, 1997; Ottman, 1998). Consumer behaviour and decision making are interdisciplinary in nature. Consumer behaviour focuses on how individuals make decisions to spend their available resources on consumption-related items. In light of the above factors the study analyzes impact of Environmental Concern on the Consumption of Eco-friendly products.

1.7. Limitations of the Study

This study does not claim to respondent view of all consumers throughout India as the respondents were chosen purposively from Coimbatore city. Model used in this study was tested for eco- friendly product purchase with selected factors identified from literature and did not explore the factors not quoted in the literature. Any other alternative results regarding the consumption of eco – friendly products, if any beyond the scope of research.

1.8. Chapter Scheme

The study has been presented in the following five chapters

Chapter I	The first chapter deals with introduction, significance of the study, statement of the problem, objectives of the study, limitations of the study and organization of the thesis.
Chapter II	This chapter presents review of literature covering theoretical background and review of empirical studies carried out on the topic in the past.
Chapter III	This chapter discusses the research methodology adopted to conduct the study.
Chapter IV	This chapter illustrates the results and the discussion of the study. It includes Socio-economic profile of the respondents, Perception about Eco-Friendly Products Purchase, Awareness Level of Consumers about Eco-Friendly Products, Determinants influencing on consumption of eco –friendly product, Casual Relationship of determinants influencing eco-friendly products and Consumption among the respondents
Chapter V	Findings, suggestions and conclusion

CHAPTER II

2. Review of Literature

This chapter focuses on review of literature and analyze past studies related to Impact of Environmental Concern on the Consumption of Eco-Friendly Products. This chapter includes theoretical and empirical reviews from past studies.

2.1. Research Studies Pertaining to the Problem Selected

Consumption

- Shirmila Stanley (2015) conducted a study on "The Perception and Impact of Sustainable Green Consumption Practices and Women in Preserving Ecology with Special Reference to Chennai City. The aim of study was to know the awareness among women in Chennai towards green products and examine the buying motives and perception of women towards eco-friendly product. In this study they have used both primary and secondary data. Convenient sampling techniques have been used to collect the data. To analyse the data they have used percentage analysis, Annova, factor analysis and chi square analysis.
- Yatish Joshi and Zillur Rahman (2015) found in their study, "Factors Affecting Green Purchase Behaviour and Future Research Directions". This is one of the first studies that reviewed articles related to attitude - behaviour inconsistencies in the context of green purchasing. This review identified various prevalent motives, facilitators and barriers affecting purchase decision-making towards green products and provides possible explanations for inconsistencies reported in green purchase behavior. All These factors are divided into those unique to the individual decision maker and those considered situational in nature. Consumer's environmental concern and products functional attributes emerged as the two major determinants of consumer green purchase behavior. The paper informs about the main predictors of consumer's green purchase behavior. In this way, it will help policy makers and managers in formulating and implementing strategies to encourage green purchasing.
- Tan Booi Chen et al., (2010) found in their study on "Attitude towards the Environment and Green Products: Consumers' Perspective". This paper is essentially exploratory in nature and has two objectives. The first objective is to compare gender with attitudes towards the environment and green products. The second objective is to investigate the relationship between attitude towards the environment and green products. Result

from the independent sample t-test shows that there were no significant differences between gender in their environmental attitudes and attitudes on green products. The rotated factor matrix validated the underlying dimensions of environmental attitudes into three major dimensions (environmental protection, government's role, and personal norm). Results from the multiple linear regression analysis revealed that consumer attitudes on the government's role and their personal norm towards the environment contributed significantly to their attitude on green product. Further investigation revealed that personal norm was the most important contributor to the attitude towards green product. However, environmental protection did not contribute significantly to consumers' attitudes on green product.

- Magali Morel et al., (2012) conducted a study on "Green marketing: Consumers' Attitudes towards Eco-friendly Products and Purchase Intention in the Fast Moving Consumer Goods (FMCG) sector". The objective of this research was looked into and explored the influencing of four traditional marketing-mix elements, satisfaction and word of mouth (WOM) on attitude and purchasing intentions of consumers on eco-friendly products specifically fasting moving consumer goods (FMCG) or non-durable ones. A quantitative approach was adopted for the study by using a questionnaire, one paper version and another online version the total sample was composed of 174 respondents, 81 were collected through internet by using Google.doc surveys and Facebook and 93 by using standard paper questionnaire form. Indeed satisfaction goes with purchase intention. Positive attitudes concerning willingness to pay an extra price for green products are also correlated with purchase intention.
- R. Rajasekaranand et al., (2013) conducted a study on "A Study on Green Product and Innovation for Sustainable Development". The main aim of the study was to identify the significance of green product and to identify the golden roles of the green product. This study was based on secondary data. Descriptive analysis have been used to describe the collected data. This result obtained because the statistical test showed that the eco-friendly preference and eco-friendly product quality increases then implications customer satisfaction will increase. Both variables that were Eco-Friendly Preference and Eco-Friendly Product Quality have effects on their implications Customer satisfaction either partially or simultaneously.
- Preeti Sehgal (2010) conducted a study on "Impact of Eco-Friendly Products on Consumer, Behavior". The main objective of this study was to investigate the various concepts relating to eco-friendly products. This study was based on both primary and

secondary data. They have used. They have used descriptive analysis and factor analysis for analysing the collected data. Consumer choices reflect not only price and quality preferences but also social and moral values, as witnessed in the remarkable growth of the global market for organic and environmentally friendly products. In line with the halo associated with green consumerism, results showed that people act more altruistically after mere exposure to green products than after mere exposure to conventional products.

- Afzaal Ali & Israr Ahmad P (2012) conducted a study on "Environment Friendly Products: Factors that Influence the Green Purchase Intentions of Pakistani Consumers". This study examined the influence of various factors on the green purchase intentions of Pakistani consumers. To this end, a conceptual model has been proposed and subjected to empirical verification with the use of a survey. The survey results obtained in two major Pakistani cities provide reasonable support for the validity of the proposed model. Specifically, the findings from the correlation matrix, simple regression followed by multiple regression analysis confirm the influence of OGI, EK, EC and PPP&Q on consumers purchase intentions toward green products. The OGI, EK and EC, in turn, also seem to affect consumers green purchase intentions via the moderating role of PPP&Q of a green product.
- Wiwik Handayani (2017) conducted a study on "Green Consumerism: An Eco-Friendly Behaviour Form through the Green Product Consumption and Green Marketing". This research is referred to analyse the influence of consumer attitude of green product towards purchase intention. This study was based on secondary data. The result of analysis show that there is influence among consumer attitude of green product towards consumer purchase intention significantly.

Environmental Concern

- Annes Ahmad et al., (2015) conducted a study on "Consumers Intentions to Purchase Green Brands: The Role of Environmental Concern, Environmental Knowledge and Self-Expressive Benefits". The main objective of the study was to know the attitude of customer preference in green brand. This study was based on both the primary and secondary data. Structural equation model and correlation analysis have been used to analyse the data. This study found that it mainly focus on purchase experience on electronic products
- Khealo P.P et al., (2014) found in their study on "Environmental Concern, Attitude towards Green Products and Green Purchase Intentions of Consumers in Lesotho". The

main aim of the study was to know the environmental concern and attitude of green products and purchase intentions. Primary data have been used to collect the data. Regression analysis and factor analysis have been used to analyse the data.

- Grace K. Dagher et al., (2015) conducted a study on "Impact of Environmental Concern and Attitude on Green Purchasing Behavior: Gender as the Moderates", this study was based on socialization theory which suggests that individual behvaiour is shaped by gender expectation in relation to the cultural context. Their study was based on primary data. The findings revealed that green marketers could benefit from increasing the level of environmental concern an attitude among both male and female.
- Mohd Danish Kiramani et al., (2016) conducted a study on "Environmental Concern and Attitude towards Green Products: Evidence from India ". This study was conducted to find out the attitude of green products and its environmental concern in India. In this study they have used primary and secondary data to collect the data. SEM model and regression analysis were used to find out the result.
- Nargesdelafrooz at al., (2014) conducted a study on "Effects of Green Marketing on Consumer Purchase Behavior". The main aim of the study was to find out the influence of green marketing tolls such as namely, eco brand and environmental advertisement. Cluster method of sampling was used for this study. Correlation and multiple regression analysis were used to analyse the data. The result showed that environmental advertisement had the most significant effect on consumers purchasing behvaiour and eco brand had he least effect.
- Sudhirachdev (2011) conducted a study on "Eco - Friendly Products and Consumer Perception". This study covers various forms of environmentally concerned consumer behavior and their determinants. The understanding of environmentally concerned consumer behavior of importance to consumer and business in this they have used both primary and secondary data.
- Kamonthip Maichum (2017), conducted a study on "The Influence of Environmental Concern and Environmental Attitude on Purchase Intention towards Green Products: A Case Study of Young Consumers in Thailand", the main aim of the study was to investigate the influence of environmental concern and environmental attitude on purchase intention towards green products of young consumers in Thailand and the target group will be between 18-30 years old. Hence, a total of 500 questionnaires were distributed to young Thai consumers and 412 usable responses, representing a response rate of 82.40%. Data were analyzed using confirmatory factor analysis (CFA)

and structural equation modeling (SEM) was created to evaluate structural model. The findings of this study indicated that environmental concern and environmental attitude had significant positive influence on purchase intention towards green products. Moreover, the overall results have confirmed that the environmental attitude has a strongest direct influence on purchase intention. Thus, the findings could provide insights important for environmental sustainability and views of young consumers in Thailand.

Awareness

- Naazahmohdsuki (2013) conducted a study on "Green Awareness Effects on Consumers Purchasing Decision: Some insights from Malaysia". This study aims to examine the influence of consumers environmental concern, awareness of green products, price and brand image on their purchasing decision of green products. A total of 200 samples were taken for the study. Multiple regression analysis were used to analyse the data.
- Genesis Guanghai MA (2018) conducted a study on "The Effects of Environmental Awareness and Consumption Value on Green make up Product Purchase Intentions". The main objective of the study was to know the awareness level of green products. SEM model and frequency analysis were used to analyse the data.
- Christopher Gan et al., (2008) conducted a study on "Consumer Purchasing Behavior towards Green Products in New Zeeland". The main objective of the study was to find out the attitude of purchase behavior towards green products. Primary data have been used to collect the data. Probability sampling techniques have taken for sampling. percentage analysis and annova were used to analyse the data.
- Sanjeevkumar et al., (2012) conducted a study on "Consumer Awareness and Perception towards Green Product: A Study of Youngsters in India". The present study is attempted to investigate consumer perception and purchase intention towards green products among youngsters. The data have been collected through questionnaire from the youngsters in India. Frequency and f test have been used to analyse the data.
- Soegoto D.S (2018) found in their study "Analysis of Eco - Friendly Preference and Eco - Friendly Product Quality; Their Implications to Customer Satisfaction". The purpose of this study aims at analysing eco - friendly preference and eco - friendly product quality and their implications on the customer satisfaction. The research method used was quantitative method with multiple regression analysis. The result

indicated implications eco – friendly preference and eco – friendly product quality significant positive effect on customer satisfaction.

- Suganya D. (2017) conducted a study on "A Study on Consumer Awareness towards Eco-Friendly Products at Coimbatore". The main objectives of the study were to study the awareness level of eco – friendly products and buying behaviour about eco – friendly products. The Sampling technique was convenient sampling used for collecting data. To analyse the data, simple percentage and chi square method have been used. As far as consumers are concerned the awareness level is increasing and has started implementing them in their normal life and also government intervention is needed to implement normal price in green market.
- Nufazil Altaf (2013) conducted a study on "Consumers Awareness towards Green Marketing - A Study of Srinagar City". The main objective of the study was to find out the consumer awareness towards green marketing. A descriptive research was undertaken to meet the objectives of this study with the collection of both secondary and primary data. The primary data was collected from respondents in Srinagar city through a questionnaire designed for a sample of 100 respondents. In this study they have used percentage analysis to analyse the data. The current consumption levels are too high and are unsustainable. Therefore there is a need for green marketing and a need for a shift in the business organizations behavior and attitude towards providing more environmental friendly products.
- Asha P. et al., (2017) found in their study on "Consumer Awareness towards Green Products". The study brings out green product awareness among the consumers in Kanyakumari District. The main objective of this study is to know the consumer awareness about green products. The data was collected from 123 respondents. Secondary data was collected from the available literature sources. The core idea of green marketing is to create awareness among people on the environmental issues and how consumers would be helping the environment if they switch over to green products. Thus green marketing aims to provide more information to people and also gives consumers more choices to switch over to green lifestyle.
- Zillur Rahman Siddique et al., (2018) found in their study on "Sources of Consumers Awareness toward Green Products and Its Impact on Purchasing Decision in Bangladesh". This study aims to investigate the sources of consumers' awareness toward green products and its impact on purchasing decision. The data is collected from 300 respondents by survey method through a structured questionnaire with five-point

Likert scales & multiple items. Convenience and judgmental sampling method are used. Data are analysed using frequency analysis, mean, standard deviation and regression analysis. The study has found that promotional activities on eco-friendly products and reference groups significantly influence consumers green products awareness. Majority of the respondents are aware of green products. This study also reveals that green products awareness as the critical factor, which significantly affects consumers green purchasing decision. This paper can contribute to this green awareness issues. The company can be benefited knowing sources of green products awareness. Those it can aid green awareness development along with green products offer to consumer.

- Saira Yasin Lasbela, U.J. (2015) conducted a study on "Green Marketing: A Study of Consumers' Attitude towards Environment Friendly Products". This study focused on to investigates the consumers' attitude towards environment friendly products and its' impact on consumers' purchases intentions. A survey is conducted from a sample of 150 respondents selected through convenience sampling technique. The data is analyzed by employing descriptive statistics and regression analysis. The results of the study show that consumers' attitude significantly influences consumer's green buying intentions along with other major variables like eco-literacy, values, perceptions and behavior. It is found that there is great potential for environment friendly products in Pakistan consumers, as considerable number of respondents tends to be collectivistic and ecologically conscious that ensures more chances of their engagement in pro-environmental behavior and hence influencing their green purchase intentions.
- Maheswari et al., (2014) conducted a study on "Customer's attitude and awareness towards green products with reference to Coimbatore – An analytical study". The main objective of the study was to shed light on the customer's attitude, perception, and awareness and satisfaction level towards green marketing products in Coimbatore. The study was based on both primary and secondary data. For analysisng the collected data Percentage Analysis, Chi-Square Analysis, Rank and scaling techniques have been used. In this study they have found, in all over the Coimbatore city, the people and customer have awareness related to green products. Meanwhile, if the entire Coimbatore customers are became natural eco-friendly user, definitely Coimbatore will become a one of the finest clean city in future.
- Nandini Desai (2015) conducted a study on "A Study of Consumer Awareness: Towards Eco Friendly Buildings in Pune City". The main objective of the study was to find out the Consumer Perspectives on eco-friendly vs. Conventional Homes and to study the

customer awareness level amongst the customers. In this study, for collecting primary data, the survey method of data collection was used. The data was collected through structured personal interview method and to some extend observational method was also incorporate for data collection. It found that, Green constructions from residential estates to Malls and airports should be considered in the long term strategy plan as a long term solution to combat climate change and reduce utilization of fossil fuels and reduce wastage of water.

- Preeti Pillai et al., (2015) found in their study on "A Study on Consumers' Perception towards Eco-friendly Products in Ahmedabad". This paper aimed to understand the perception of consumers towards eco -friendly white goods, awareness about the availability of such products and the demographic profile of green consumers. Tis study was based on primary data. The data for this study was collected through the distribution of self-administered questionnaires via online method (e-mail) and offline method (hand delivery) to potential respondents across Ahmedabad. For analysing the collected data, descriptive analysis technique have been used. The findings of the study clearly confirm that respondents do not have very favorable perception towards eco-friendly products.

Satisfaction

- Ranjithkumar M.S et al., (2018) conducted in their study "A Study on Consumers Level of Satisfaction towards Eco-Friendly Products". The main objective of the study was to know the satisfaction level of eco - friendly products and to find out the environmental problems. Primary data have been used to collect the data namely convenient sampling method. To analyse the data, percentage analysis and ranking analysis were used. As the consumers are looking for branded products it is the responsibility of the producers that they should be more concerned for environmentally sound products.
- Meenakshi Saratha M. (2015) conducted "A study on Customer Satisfaction Level on Green Products with Special Reference to Coimbatore District". The main aim of the study was to find the customers willingness to buy green products in Coimbatore district and to find the satisfaction level of the existing products which the customers use. The Sampling design used for the research was non probabilistic convenient sampling. In this study they have used Kolmogorov-Smirnov test, Mann-Whitney test and Kruskal-Wallis test for analysing the collected data. It is clearly evident from review of literature and the conceptual model that the majority of the consumers still lack 'green' knowledge and because of such low awareness towards green products,

organizations are still not pushing towards developing more green products nor are they working hard on green packaging.

- Soegoto D.S (2018) found in their study "Analysis of Eco - Friendly Preference and Eco - Friendly Product Quality; Their Implications to Customer Satisfaction". The purpose of this study is to analyse eco - friendly preference and eco - friendly product quality and their implications on the customer satisfaction. The research method used was quantitative method with multiple regression analysis. The result indicated implications that include eco - friendly preference and eco - friendly product quality has a significant positive effect on customer satisfaction.
- Anu Varghese et al (2015), conducted "A Study on Consumer Perception on Eco - Friendly Products with Reference to Kollam District in Kerala". The main aim of the study was to comprehend the consumer awareness of eco - friendly products and analyse the factors behind the preference of their selected products. The study was designed as descriptive in nature based on the survey method. Both primary and secondary data was used for the study. Nowadays, eco - friendly products are readily available, and one can be earth friendly by using these products. Environmental sustainability has become an essential ingredient to pursue business responsibly and successfully.
- Parthiban V.N (2016), conducted a study on "Consumer Perception towards the Green Marketing: A Study with Special Reference to Chennai City". The objective of the study was to study the awareness about the green marketing among the consumers in Chennai city and to evaluate the factors which enhances green products attractiveness to consumers in Chennai city. To fulfil the above objectives, 200 questionnaires were distributed and collected from the consumers in Chennai city. Out of which 12 samples were ejected due to inadequate information provided by the consumers. Finally, 188 samples finalized for the study. The data collected from the respondents was tested with suitable statistical techniques. Demographic background of respondents and customer awareness about green marketing system were analyzed by taking percentage analysis. Further chi-square test and Friedman test were used.
- Suresh Kumar D. (2015) conducted a study on "A Study of Consumers' Perception and Attitude towards Green Products". The main aim of the study was to study the relationship between socio economic characteristics of consumers and perception and attitude towards green products. Primary data have been used to collect the data. For analysing the collected data, descriptive analysis and chi - square test have been used.

It is observed that the consumer's these days are more aware about green marketing. People in emerging economics like India too have high concern for greener environment and have an overall positive attitude towards green marketing.

- Bambang Supriadi et al., (2017) conducted a study on "Green Product and its Impact on Customer Satisfaction". This study was conducted to analyze the influence of green products towards customer satisfaction in improving environment-based occupancy hotels. The respondents for this study were 130 respondents who had been picked up randomly to make the questionnaire easier to answer. The data were collected and analyzed by using Statistic Program Social Sciences (SPSS). The tests used for analysis were independent t-test and simple regression analysis. The estimation of the regression equation tested partially by using t-test.
- Zainabzurfiquar (2015), conducted a study on "Green Marketing: Environmental Concern and Customer Satisfaction". The objective of the study was to know the awareness level of green marketing and green products. Quantitative technique has been adopted thereby using the questionnaire method. The findings of the study showed that people are less aware about the importance of green products.

Research Gap

The studies reviewed above indicated that concern over the environment in the form of consumer's consumption impacts environmental friendly products. On the basis of the above reviews, many earlier studies were neglected to investigate the impact of Environmental Concern on the Consumption of eco-friendly products. As consumers become aware of the consequences of their consumer behaviour, they can experience feelings of guilt which motivates them towards eco-friendly consumption. These areas are most favoured destinations for this study to identify the impact of environmental concern on the consumption of eco-friendly products.

Information from the consumer research is being used to develop new products and to redesign existing products in order to reduce environmental impact. The social pressure on business has indicated that green marketing necessitates providing consumers with more sustainable and socially acceptable products. Therefore eco - friendly products consumption must involve consuming in a more sustainable and socially responsible way.

CHAPTER III

3. Research Methodology

3.1. Introduction

This chapter focuses on the research approach, design and methodology procedures used in the study. The research for the present study is descriptive and analytical in nature. The research methodology inculcated in this study includes the following aspects namely development of interview schedule (questionnaire), the various methods followed during data collection and statistical techniques applied to test hypotheses.

3.2. Development of Conceptual Framework

The conceptual framework provides a focus and direction to the study. The various variables and expected associations can be clearly understood by developing a conceptual framework. Based on both the literature review and theory of planned behaviour, a theoretical frame has been proposed to predict respondents' green products purchase decision.

Table 3.1: Conceptual Framework - Satisfaction of the Eco-Friendly Products Derived as a Factor Influenced by Consumption of Eco-Friendly Products

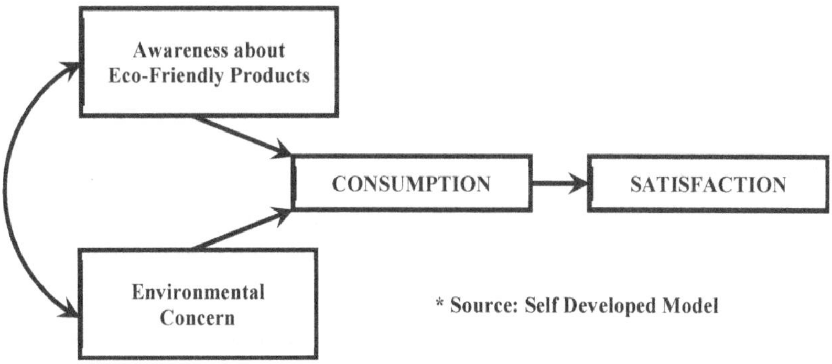

* **Source: Self Developed Model**

3.2.1. Awareness about Eco-Friendly Products

Knowledge of the environmental impacts of products production leads to concern for the environment, which in turn leads to environmentally friendly consumption behavior, Deborah (2010). Consumers aware are about impact of buying activity on environment and majority of the consumers are aware about the consumption of eco- friendly products, Sarang Bhola (2014). (Awareness of customers about eco-friendly products- a study of, Satara district). Consumption experiences can influence behaviour awareness, Triantafillidou and Siomkos (2014) and consumers becoming more familiar with eco- friendly products could influence awareness towards eco – friendly products among the consumers. Green Advertising communicates benefits of losing eco- friendly products to the society, Chang (2011). Unfamiliarity with the green product may cause less interested to consume the eco- friendly product, Glegg et al (2005). Changes of buying behaviours are also occurred because of eco – friendly product awareness, Ottaman (1993). ***Based on this awareness about Eco-friendly products derived as an influencing factor and it may affect consumption of Eco-Friendly products.***

3.2.2. Environmental Concern

People are aware of environmental problems and they readiness to contribute personally to their solutions by the consumption of eco- friendly products, Dulnap Jones (2002). The awareness regarding the environmental concern have a positive behaviour of the consumers, Roberts (1996). The increased knowledge about the environmental issues creates positive consumption towards eco- friendly products, Arcury (1990). Knowledge about the environmental problems can make individuals ore responsible towards the environment, Schahn and Holzer (1990). Consumers who are more aware and conscious about the environment make more consumption towards the eco – friendly products, Birgelen et al., (2009). Based on these reviews it can be identified that the consumers who have more aware about the environmental issues are more likely to go for eco- friendly purchases. ***Based on these reviews concern about environment derived as an influencing factor and it may affect consumption of Eco-Friendly products.***

3.2.3. Consumption on Eco-Friendly Products

According to Carrigan et al (2004), Green consumption is related not only to consuming goods without damage to the natural environment, but also to buying environmentally friendly products and to recycling. In understanding green consumption, the concept of green products also needs clarifying. Green products (eco-products or environmentally friendly products) are considered as products that do not pollute the earth or damage natural resources and can be recycled or conserved, Shamdasani et al (1993). William Young et al. (2010), analyzed that incentives and single issue labels would help consumers to concentrate their purchasing behaviour in green products. Pavan Mishra and Payal Sharma (2010), Consumers are willing to pay more to maintain a cleaner and greener environment and marketers also have responsibility to make the consumers understand the need and benefits of green products. Mahesh and Ganapathi (2012), Consumers who have a higher monthly income and educational qualification are more likely to be concerned about the environment and therefore tend to purchase green products. ***Based on these reviews Consumption of Eco-Friendly Products derived as a factor may influence by awareness and environmental concern of Eco-Friendly products.***

3.2.4. *Satisfaction*

Satisfaction is a person's feeling of pleasure and disappointment. Resulting from consumption of products Kotler and Keller (2009). Furthermore the customer satisfaction is the attitude of the overall assessment of a good are service after purchase and use. Eco - friendly product quality and product preference have effects on their implications customer satisfaction partially, Soegoto (2018). Eco - friendly products positively and significantly influence the customer satisfaction. Bambang Supriai (2017). The opinion of the customer satisfaction is a comparison between what is expected and what is obtained. A consumers' purchase behaviour depends on the consumers' satisfaction towards the eco- friendly product and it is mostly influenced by the attributes of the eco- friendly products, Ursil Majid (2016). Customers' satisfaction towards particular product will influence the future consumption decisions of consumers, Oliver (1999). And a satisfied consumer is going to repeat his consumption in future, Zeithaml et al., (1996). ***Based on these reviews Satisfaction of the Eco-Friendly Products derived as a factor influenced by consumption of Eco-Friendly products.***

3.3. Research Hypotheses

Based on the conceptual model framed by the researcher, the following hypotheses have been developed.

- **H_1:** A significant relationship exists between Awareness about Eco-Friendly Products of the respondents and Eco-Friendly Products Consumption of the respondents.
- **H_2:** A significant relationship exists between Environmental Concern of the respondents and Eco-Friendly Products Consumption of the respondents.
- **H_3:** A significant relationship exists between Eco-Friendly Products Consumption of the respondents and Satisfaction of Eco-Friendly products consumption.
- **H_4:** A significant relationship exists between Awareness on eco-friendly products and concern on environment

3.4. Research Methodology

Coimbatore city in Coimbatore district has been selected as the locale of the study, owing to the reason that the district is one among the industrially developed and commercially vibrant districts of Tamilnadu. The study is both descriptive and analytical in nature. The respondents are being selected on the basis of particular characteristics of the population and the interest in a specific field. A well structured interview schedule will be prepared and administered among the respondents to obtain primary data. Proposed sample size of the study is 200, and further statistical test will be carried out after testing the reliability of the data collected.

3.5. Locale of the Study

Coimbatore city in Coimbatore district has been selected as the locale of the study, owing to the reason that the district is one among the industrially developed and commercially vibrant districts of Tamilnadu. Coimbatore is the third largest city in Tamilnadu and the 14th largest in India. Coimbatore city is a district head quarter. According to the census 2011, the total population of Coimbatore district is 34,72,578. The Coimbatore city has total population of 10,50,721 of which 5,26,163 are male and 5,24,558 are female, of which 26,33,170 is the urban population and 8,39,408 includes the rural population. Coimbatore is called "the Manchester of South India" and it has been identified as one of the fast developing metros in India. Coimbatore city has been included in the list of smart cities.

Coimbatore Solid Waste Management Project under Jawaharlal Nehru National Urban Renewal Mission (JNNURM) brought a wave of change in the Solid Waste Management (SWM) practices in the city. Recycling and Reusing of waste has increased by 60 per cent which is a significant positive impact of the project on the city's environment by effective diversion of waste from landfills.

A spurt in the growth of shops dealing with environmentally sustainable products is also evidenced at all zones of the city. These initiatives bring the awareness of environmental impact and environmental concern to the residents. In response to their collective efforts, the message of eco-friendly lifestyle is being spread across the city on a steady welcoming pace. There is a certain degree of awareness about environment protection and greener lifestyle among the residents of the city.

3.6. Research Method

The present study is both descriptive and analytical in nature. The descriptive research allows the researcher to measure and report the occurrence with which specific variable occur in the sample to present an image of the facts of a condition or relationship. Similarly the analytical research usually concerns itself with cause-effect relationships. The research objectives and hypotheses are focused on establishing a causal relationship and quantitative data collection, and analyses methods are well suitable for studying the relationship.

3.7. Population and Sampling Strategy

The population for the study consisted of customers who bought any of the green products available in the study area. Though there are a number of products in terms of eco-friendliness, the products which are commonly available in Coimbatore city include the green or environment friendly products, eco-friendly carry bags or plates or cups, recycled papers and or stationeries, energy efficient lamps, solar products, fruits, vegetables, dairy products, organic food available detergent powder and personal care products. Of them, consumers with an awareness and consumption on purchase of eco-friendly products have been consciously selected for the present study.

3.8. Determining the Sample Size

The total number of sample respondents drawn from the study area is 200. Due to terminating the interview in progress and unwillingness to provide complete the data by few respondents, total sample size of 169 respondents has finally resulted in.

3.9. Sampling Method

A Purposive sampling method has been adopted in the study. The study aimed at analyzing the urban consumer consumption towards eco-friendly products and Coimbatore has been consciously selected. The respondents have been identified from a number of shops dealing with the eco-friendly products and green shops in the city. The respondents purchasing eco-friendly products have been selected.

3.10. Sources of Data Collection

Both primary and secondary data were collected and used in this study. The primary data collection is made through interview schedule, a method of data collection which can be administered by interviewers in person. The secondary data required for the study are collected from the standard text books, previous studies, journal article, reports, records and websites.

3.11. Primary Data Collection Tool and Measures

The primary data were collected through a well-structured interview schedule. It was framed based on measurement namely Awareness and environmental concern which were derived based on the earlier research which were presented on a five points Likert Scale, used to identify the influence of respondents' consumption leading towards satisfaction for Eco-friendly products.

3.12. Collection of Data

The primary data for the study were collected during the period between January 2019 to February 2019.

3.13. Framework of Analysis

Further statistical test were carried out, after testing the reliability of the data collected.

- ***Frequency Distribution (Percentage Analysis)***

The **Frequency Distribution (Percentage Analysis)** was used to know the distribution pattern of respondents with respect to variables. The Frequency Distributions of the variables were calculated with the help of simple percentage, by writing the formula;

$$\textbf{Percentage} = \frac{\textbf{Frequency (F)}}{\textbf{Number of Respondents (N)}} \textbf{ X 100}$$

** **Where; Frequency (F) → Number of Respondents; Number of Respondents (N) → Total Number of Sample Population***

- ***Measures of Central Tenancy (Mean)***

The **Mean** is a single value calculated from a group of values to represent them in a simple way. The average obtained by dividing the sum of the data by the number of data in the set. Given a set of data, $\{x_1, x_2, x_3, ..., x_n\}$, you can find the mean, $\bar{x}$, using the following formula:

$$\bar{x} = \frac{x_1 + x_2 + x_3 + ... + x_n}{n} \quad (or)\ \bar{x} = \frac{1}{n}\sum_{i=1}^{n} x_i$$

- ***Measures of Dispersion (Standard Deviation)***

The extent to which, the data differs from the mean value (average). The standard deviation is a measure of how the data is clustered about the mean. For large sets of data, approximately 68.3% of the data lies within one standard deviation of the mean and approximately 95.4% of the data lies within two standard deviations of the mean.

$$\sigma = \sqrt{\frac{(x_1 - \bar{x})^2 + (x_2 - \bar{x})^2 + (x_3 - \bar{x})^2 + ... + (x_n - \bar{x})^2}{n}}$$

$$= \sqrt{\frac{\sum_{i=1}^{n}(x_i - \bar{x})^2}{n}}$$

- ***Analysis of Variance***

The ANOVA is designed to test whether a significant difference exists among the two or more sample means. The purpose of Analysis of Variance (ANOVA) is to test the significant differences between means. The interest lies in testing the null hypothesis that the category means are equal in the population. In other words,

$$H_0: \mu_1 = \mu_2 = \mu_3 \ldots\ldots\ldots = \mu_c$$

Under the null hypothesis, SS_x and SS_{error} come from the same source of variation. In such a case, the estimate of the population variance of Y can be based on either 'between category' variation or 'within-category' variation. In other words, the estimate of the population variance of Y,

$$S_y^2 = SS_x / (c\text{-}1) = \text{mean square due to X} = MS_x$$

$$S_y^2 = SS_{error} / (N\text{-}c) = \text{mean square due to error} = MS_{error}$$

$$F = SS_x / (c\text{-}1) / SS_{error} / (N\text{-}c) = MS_x / MS_{error}$$

The null hypothesis may be tested by the F statistics based on the ratio between these two estimates with (c-1) and (N-c) degrees of freedom (df). One-way ANOVA tests the differences in a single interval dependent variable among two, three, or more groups formed by the categories of a single categorical independent variable. Also known as univariate ANOVA, simple ANOVA, single classification ANOVA, or one-factor ANOVA, this design deals with one independent variable and one dependent variable.

In this study, the total variance in a set of data is divided into variation within groups and variation between groups. The ANOVA technique is based on the concept of sum squared deviations from a mean. In this study, ANOVA is applied to test whether there is any significant difference between the mean value of selected constructs in influencing green products purchase behaviour and the socio-economic profile of the urban respondents.

- **Factor analysis** – Factor analysis is a technique used when there is a systematic interdependence among a set of observed variables and for finding out something more fundamental or latent which creates communality.
- **Factor** – A factor is an underlying dimension of several related variables. There can be one or more factors in a phenomenon depending upon its nature and the number variables involved in it.
- **Factor Loadings** – These are values which explain how closely the variables are related to each other of the factors discovered. They are factor variable correlations. It is the absolute size of loading that is important in the interpretation of factors.

- **Communality (h^2)** - It shows how much of each variable is accounted for by the underlying factors taken together. A high degree of communality means that not much of the variable is left over after whatever the factors represent is taken into consideration.
- **Eigen Value or Latent Root** - When the sum of squared values of factor loadings relating to a factor is taken, then such sum is referred to as Eigen value or latent root. Eigen value indicates the relative importance of each factor in accounting for a particular set of variables being analyzed.
- **Rotation** - Rotation in factor analysis is something like staining a micro scope slide. The rotation option selected is Varimax rotation. Varimax rotation tries to find cluster of items that go together and that can be differentiated from other clusters. It also assumes that factors are Orthogonal. Varimax rotation maximizes (simultaneously for all factors) the variance of the loadings within each factor. The variance of a factor is largest when its smallest loadings tend towards zero and its largest loadings tend towards unity. In essence, the solution obtained through Varimax rotation produces factors that are characterized by large loadings on relatively few variables.
- **Number of Factors** -The criteria used are those factors whose Eigen vales are greater than one (Kaiser Criterion) which has been selected for analysis.
- **Interpretation of factors** - The variables, whose factor loading is greater than 0.5 were considered significant among the factors, and these variables were grouped as one as they were similar in nature and renamed as factor.
- In this study, factor analysis was used to identify the purchase behaviour of respondents towards green products on the basis of lifestyle and for the association of constructs to identify the green products purchase behaviour.
- **Garrett Ranking Technique** - To find out the most significant factor which influences the respondent, Garrett's ranking technique was used. As per this method, respondents have been asked to assign the rank for all factors and the outcome of such ranking has been converted into score value with the help of the following formula:

$$\textbf{Percentage Proportion} = \frac{\mathbf{100(R_{ij} - 0.5)}}{\mathbf{N_j}}$$

Where, R_{ij} = Rank given for the ith variable by j^{th} respondents; N_j= Number of variable ranked by j^{th} respondents

With the help of Garrett's Table, the percent position estimated is converted into scores. Then for each factor, the scores of each individual are added and then total value of scores and mean values of score is calculated. The factors having highest mean value is considered to be the most important factor.

3.14. Operational Definitions of the Concepts Used in the Study

- **Environmental Concern** - Environmental concern as an affective environmental attitude (e.g. Schultz et al. 2004, 2005). Affective attitudes referring to the seriousness and importance of environmental problems.
- Knowledge or perception of a situation or fact.
- **Consumption** - Consumption in its simplest sense is the possession and use of goods and services, Robert East (2008).
- **Satisfaction** - Satisfaction means as meeting consumer expectations and it described as contentment, Oliver (1989).
- **Eco-Friendly Product** - A green product is one which should not endanger the health of people or animals and damage the environment at any stage of its life, including manufacture, use and disposal, John Elleington (2019). Products, those are manufactured through green technology and that caused no environmental hazards are called green products, Verma (2012).
- **Green Marketing** - Green marketing, also known as environmental marketing and sustainable marketing, refers to an organization's efforts at designing, promoting, pricing and distributing products that will not harm the environment, Pride and Ferrel (1993).

3.15. Ethical Consideration

The researcher ensured that the information provided by the respondents will be kept secret and confidential. The information will be used for the academic and research purpose only. The researcher did not collect any personal information such as name, employee code and contact details from the participants.

3.16. Summary

This chapter describes about the introduction to the research methods, research design and sampling method adopted in this study. The research instruments (interview schedule) for the study (satisfaction of the eco-friendly products derived as a factor influenced by consumption of eco-friendly products) were adopted. The data collection methods from the sample respondents and statistical tools applied for the analysis of data are also included in this chapter.

CHAPTER IV

4. Results and Discussion

The results of the study on "**An Overview of Consumers' Awareness towards Eco-Friendly Products**" is presented under the following heads:

4.1. Socio-economic profile of the respondents

4.2. Perception of Eco-Friendly Products Purchase

4.2.1. Usage of Eco-friendly products

4.2.2. Motive to use the Eco-friendly products

4.2.3. Sources of knowledge about Eco-friendly products

4.2.4. Preferred place of purchase of Eco-friendly products

4.2.5. Regularity of purchase of Eco-friendly products

4.2.6. Eco-friendly products prices are higher

4.2.7. Consideration of environment before purchasing of Eco-friendly products

4.2.8. Eco-labeled products change the choice of purchase

4.2.9. Consideration of recycled products and packages before purchase

4.2.10. Trust the quality of Eco-friendly products

4.2.11. Aware of purchasing Eco-friendly products will contribute to the sustainable development

4.2.12. Marketing strategies influencing purchase behaviour of Eco-friendly products

4.3. Awareness Level of Consumers about Eco-Friendly Products

4.4. Determinants influencing on consumption of eco–friendly product

4.5. Relationship of influencing factors towards eco-friendly products Consumption among the respondents

4.1. Socio-economic Profile of the Respondents

Socio-economic profile determines consumers' requirements for products and the potential to buy them. It is the simple and coherent way to classify people and can be assessed more accurately than the other. The following table exhibits the socio-economic profile of the respondents.

Table 4.1: Socio-economic Profile of the Respondents

Variables	Frequency N (169)	Percentage %
Age		
Up to 25 years	50	29.6
26-50 years	66	39.1
Above 50 years	53	31.4
Gender		
Male	55	32.5
female	114	67.5
Marital status		
Married	107	63.3
Unmarried	62	36.7
Educational status		
Up to school	84	49.7
UG	66	39.1
PG	12	7.1
Profession	7	4.1
Occupation		
Govt. employee	19	11.2
Private employee	54	32.0
Business/Profession	13	7.7
Others	83	49.1
Monthly Income		
Up to Rs.10,000	84	49.7
From Rs.10,001 to Rs.25,000	59	34.9
Above Rs.25,000	26	15.4
Nature of family		
Joint family	28	16.6
Nuclear family	141	83.4
No. of family members		
Up to 3	25	14.8
4-6	131	77.5
above 6	13	7.7
No. of earning members		
One member	99	58.6
2 members	59	34.9
above 2 members	11	6.5

Source: Computed data

The need for the product may vary with consumers' age, and it is a key factor in the consumption of many products. The above table illustrates that, 29.6 per cent of the respondents belong to the age category of up to 25 years, 39.1 per cent of the respondents belong to 26-50 years and 31.4 per cent of the respondents belong to the age category of above 50 years.

Gender based analysis is being explored by marketers in India. It is observed from the above table that, 32.5 per cent of the respondents are male and 67.5 per cent of the respondents are female. In general, products and services are exclusively designed for male and female.

Marital status is an important phenomenon used for marketing the products. The above table shows that 63.3 per cent of the respondents are married and 36.7 per cent of the respondents are unmarried.

It is found that, 49.7 per cent of the respondents belong to the category of up to school level, 39.1 per cent of the respondents belong to under graduates, 7.1 per cent of the respondents belong to post graduates and 4.1 per cent of the respondents belong to the category of profession.

In terms of occupation, 11.2 per cent of the respondents are government employees, 32.0 per cent of the respondents are private employees and 7.7 per cent of the respondents belong to the category of business/profession and the remaining 49.1 per cent of the respondents belong to the occupational category of others.

As far as monthly income is concerned, 49.7 per cent of the respondents belong to the category of up to Rs. 10,000 and 34.9 per cent of the respondents' monthly income is from Rs. 10,001 to Rs. 25,000 and 15.4 per cent of the respondents belong to the category of above Rs. 25,000. Income is an important variable for distinguishing between market segments because it indicates an ability or inability to pay for a product or brand.

Each and every family needs different products and services for their use. It is observed that, 16.6 per cent of the respondents belong to joint family and 83.4 per cent of the respondents belong to nuclear family.

In terms of number of family members, 14.8 per cent of the respondents belong to the category of up to 3 members, 77.5 per cent of the respondents belong to the category of 4-6 members and 7.7 per cent of the respondents belong to the category of above 6 members.

In case of number of earning members in the family, 58.6 per cent of the respondents belong to the category of 1 earning member, 34.9 per cent of the respondents belong to the category of 2 members and 6.5 per cent of the respondents belong to the category of above 2 members.

4.2. Perception about of Eco-Friendly Products Purchase

In order to understand the Eco-Friendly Products purchase, the factors such as usage, motive to use, sources of awareness, preferred place of purchase, regularity of purchase, agreement of respondents about eco-friendly products prices are higher, consideration of environment before purchasing of eco-friendly products, eco-labelled products change the choice of purchase, consideration of recycled products and packages before purchase, trust on the quality of eco-friendly products, awareness towards purchasing eco-friendly products will contribute to the sustainable development, reasons for not using eco-friendly products and marketing strategies influencing the purchase behaviour of eco-friendly products have been considered. The following table consists of understanding the purchase of Eco-Friendly products.

Table 4.2: Perception about of Eco-Friendly Products Purchase

Products	No. of Respondents	Percentage
Usage of Eco-friendly products		
Organic food	135	79.88
Organic clothes	6	3.55
Cosmetics and personal care products	12	7.10
Electrical appliances	16	9.47
Motive to use the Eco-friendly products		
Concern for Health	58	34.32
Concern for status	13	7.69
Concern for the environment	65	38.46
To use better quality products	33	19.53
Sources of awareness about Eco-friendly products		
T.V	102	38.46
Magazines	17	10.06
Internet Ads	36	6.51
Friends/ Relatives	25	20.12
Newspaper	20	11.83
Seminars/Conferences	14	8.28
Super Market staff	7	4.73
Preferred place of purchase of Eco-friendly products		
Retail Malls	33	19.53
Local shops	71	42.01
Internet	3	1.78
Teleshopping	4	2.37
Specialized shops/units	57	33.73
Factory Outlet	1	0.59
Regularity of purchase of Eco-friendly products		
Once a Week	59	34.91
Fortnight	8	4.73
Once in a Month	51	30.18
Once in a Year	6	3.55
Regularly when needed	45	26.63
Eco-friendly products prices are higher		
Yes	121	71.60
No	48	28.40
Consideration of environment before purchasing of Eco-friendly products		
Yes	151	89.35
No	18	10.65
Eco-labeled products change the choice of purchase		
Yes	162	95.86
No	7	4.14
Consideration of recycled products and packages before purchase		
Yes	143	84.62
No	26	15.38
Trust the quality of Eco-friendly products		
Yes	133	78.70
No	36	21.30
Aware of purchasing Eco-friendly products will contribute to the sustainable development		
Yes	159	94.08
No	10	5.92

Source: Computed data

4.2.1. *Usage of Eco-Friendly Products*

Usage of eco-friendly products reduces negative effect on health (Kenpetti). The table shows that majority (79.88 per cent) of the sample respondents uses organic food, 9.47 per cent of the sample respondents use Electrical appliances, 7.10 per cent of the sample respondents use cosmetics and personal care product and 3.55 per cent of the products use organic clothes.

4.2.2. *Motivation to use Eco-Friendly Products*

Motivation is the state of drive or arousal that propels behaviour towards a goal. It may be referred as the state of mind that energizes and directs goal oriented behaviour (Srabanti Mukherjee, 2012).

Table 4.2 depicts that 38.46 per cent of the respondents have the concern on environment which motive them to use the eco-friendly products, 34.32 per cent have the concern for health, 19.53 per cent have the motive to use better quality products and 7.69 per cent have status as the motive to use the eco-friendly products.

4.2.3. *Sources of Awareness about Eco-friendly Products*

Apart from this, an attempt was made to identify the effectiveness of various sources providing the information about eco - friendly products. An important communications challenge for green advertisers is to help their customers to make the links between the causes and effects of environmental and social problems. Sales promotions aim to increase sales and consumption (Ken Peattie, 1995).

It is observed from the table that 38.46 per cent of the respondents have got awareness about eco-friendly products from Television followed by friendly/relatives (20.12 per cent), newspaper (11.83 per cent), magazines (10.06 per cent), seminars/conferences (8.23 per cent), internet ads (6.51) and super market staff (4.73 per cent).

4.2.4. *Preferred Place of Purchase of Eco-Friendly Products*

Availability of products and price of the products can influence the preferred place of purchase of eco-friendly products.

It is apparent from the above table that 42.01 per cent of the sample respondents purchase eco-friendly products at local shops, 33.73 per cent purchase at specialize shops/units, 19.53 per cent of the sample respondents at retail malls, 2.37 per cent of the sample respondents at teleshopping, 1.78 per cent of the sample respondents purchase through internet and 0.59 per cent of the sample respondents at factory outlet.

4.2.5. Regularity of Purchase of Eco-Friendly Products

Method of pricing can also determine the extent and nature of product usage, such as weekly and monthly. This can influence other purchase decisions. The fairness of pricing has been a key issue for the consumer movement (Ken Peattie, 1995).

The table clearly indicates that34.91 per cent of the sample respondents purchase eco-friendly products once a week, followed by once in a month (30.18 per cent), regularly when needed (26.63 per cent), fortnight (4.73 per cent) and once in a year (3.55 per cent).

4.2.6. Eco-Friendly Products Prices are Higher

Increasing evidence of environmental degradation is bringing home to consumers that the price of consumption is not simply a monetary one. For some products their prices will increasingly be determined by their scarcity (Ken Peattie, 1995). As natural resources become scarce, the demand will begin to exceed supply and both these factors will push prices up.

The Table indicates that 71.60 per cent of the sample respondents have agreed that the eco-friendly products prices are higher whereas 28.40 per cent of the sample respondents did not agree with this statement.

4.2.7. Consideration of Environment before Purchasing of Eco-Friendly Products

Packaging has become a particular focus of green concern. The packaging of a product offers opportunity for improving the environmental performance of the tangible product. If a product is over packaged, it is unnecessarily using scarce natural resources, consuming energy and creating unnecessary waste. There are number of waste which a marketer can reduce while packaging consumed by a product without compromising the primary performance of the product or a packaging (Ken Peattie, 1995).

The table 4.2 advocates that 89.35 per cent of the sample respondent consider environment before purchasing eco-friendly products whereas 10.65 per cent of the sample respondents do not consider the environment.

4.2.8. Eco-Labelled Products Change the Choice of Purchase

India's Central Pollution Control Board has an eco-mark scheme, wherein Eco-mark label is mainly provided to manufacturers of organic and eco-friendly products and it signifies that the product which carries it does the least damage to the environment.

The table indicates that 95.86 per cent of the sample respondents change their choice of purchase eco-friendly products when they are seeing eco-labelled whereas 4.14 per cent of the sample respondents do not change their choice.

4.2.9. Consideration of Recycled Products and Packages before Purchase

Packaging consumption can also be reduced if consumers are encouraged to reuse packaging. Super markets are encouraging consumers to use less plastic shopping bags by selling sturdy reusable bags or offering a penny refunds for consumers that reuse plastic bags. Glass bottles for milk and other beverages are the most traditional reusable packaging. A bottle needs to make ten strips to become cost effective in energy saving.

Recycling can produce major saving in both material and energy. Packaging materials that cannot be directly recycled and can be indirectly recycled by transformation into another useful material. Packaging material can also be created from the recycling of other material. Only a small proportion of recyclable packaging material is recycled (Larson, 1990).

The table illustrates that 84.62 per cent of the sample respondents consider products and packages are designed to be recycled while purchasing products whereas 15.38 per cent of the sample respondents do not consider the same.

4.2.10. Trust the Quality of Eco-Friendly Products

Price consciousness is that influences on response to quality of product. Price differences within a given market and the degree to which the market involves standard or generally accepted price level and ranges are studied.

The table depicts that 78.70 per cent of the sample respondents trust the quality while purchasing of eco-friendly product whereas 21.30 per cent of the sample respondents do not trust.

4.2.11. Aware of Purchasing Eco-Friendly Products will Contribute to the Sustainable Development

Sustainable development is as the process of development which meets the needs of the present generation without compromising the ability of future generations to meet their own needs. The package has to satisfy a variety of stakeholders. Environmentalists want minimum use of material and maximum recycling.

The table shows that 94.08 per cent of the sample respondents are aware of purchasing of eco-friendly product which will contribute to the sustainable development whereas 5.92 per cent of the sample respondents are not aware.

4.2.12. Reasons for not Using Eco-Friendly Products

In order to analyse the reason for the customers not using eco-friendly products, seven reasons have been identified and considered for the analysis. Garratt's ranking has been used in this regards and the result is displayed in the following table.

4.2.13. Marketing Strategies Influencing Purchase Behaviour of Eco-Friendly Products

In this section, an attempt is made to analyse the marketing strategies influencing the purchase behaviour of eco-friendly products by using Garrett's ranking analysis. Six strategies have been identified and used in this analysis. The result is presented in the following table.

Table 4.3: Marketing Strategies Influencing Purchase Behaviour of Eco-Friendly Products: Garratt's Ranking Analysis

Marketing Strategy	**Mean score**	**Rank**
Advertisements using Green Themes	52.09	III
Offer a free gift with every product	51.19	IV
Self-Explanatory Labels	53.25	II
Certifications	57.08	I
Educational Campaigns	48.59	V
Create an explainer video	47.80	VI

Source: Computed data

The table 4.3 shows that Certifications is the main strategy with the mean score of 57.08 followed by Self Explanatory Labels (53.25), Advertisements using Green Themes (52.09), free gift offer with every product (51.19), Educational Campaigns (48.59) and Create an explainer video (47.80).

Hence, it is concluded that Certifications on eco-friendly product is the main marketing strategy that would influence the purchase behaviour of eco-friendly products.

4.3. Awareness Level of Consumers about Eco-Friendly Products

In order to analyze the Awareness level of consumers about Eco-Friendly products, 11 products have been considered. They are Reusable Coffee Cups, Stainless steel Drink Bottles, Eco-friendly Bags, Beauty products, Household appliances, Eco-Friendly Furniture, Eco-friendly paints, Solar products, Paper products, Cleaning products and Organic Fruits and vegetables.

Major determinants impact consumer Awareness and further it leads them to buy green products (Manveerkaur, 2018). Knowledge about eco-friendly products is indifferent from the demographic variables (Preeti Pillai, 2013). Usage of green product will help them to deviate their life style into a green one. But the awareness level on the usage of green products among the people is very limited (Asha, 2017).

Relationship between Personal and Socio Economic Variables and the Level of Awareness of the Sample Respondents about Eco-Friendly Products

The identified personal and socio economic variable, which might influence the level of awareness about Eco-friendly products, are as follows:

1. Age
2. Gender
3. Marital Status
4. Educational Status
5. Nature of occupation
6. Monthly Income
7. Nature of family
8. Number of family members
9. Number of earning members

Significance of the relationship among the above variables with the awareness about the Eco-friendly products has been analyzed by applying F-test and Z-test.

The following table shows the awareness level of consumers about Eco-Friendly products based on their socio-economic profile.

Table 4.4: Relationship between Personal and Socio Economic Variables and the Awareness of the Sample Respondents about Eco-Friendly Products

	N	% of Total N	Sum	Mean	F	Sig.
Age						
Upto 25	50	29.6%	859.00	17.1800	4.612	.011*
26 to 40	66	39.1%	1157.00	17.5303		
above 40	53	31.4%	962.00	18.1509		
Gender						
Male	55	32.5%	980.00	17.8182	1.055	
Female	114	67.5%	1998.00	17.5263	**Z-Value**	0.293
Marital Status						.012*
Married	107	63.3%	1912.00	17.8692	2.551	
Unmarried	62	36.7%	1066.00	17.1935	**Z-Value**	
Education						
Upto school	84	49.7%	1514.00	18.0238	6.595	.000**
UG	66	39.1%	1120.00	16.9697		
PG	12	7.1%	222.00	18.5000		
Profession	7	4.1%	122.00	17.4286		
Occupation						
Govt. employee	19	11.2%	324.00	17.0526	4.413	.005**
Private employee	54	32.0%	928.00	17.1852		
Business/Profession	13	7.7%	225.00	17.3077		
Others	83	49.1%	1501.00	18.0843		
Income						
Upto Rs.10,000	84	49.7%	1485.00	17.6786	4.724	.010*
From Rs.10,001 to Rs.25,000	59	34.9%	1015.00	17.2034		
Above Rs.25,000	26	15.4%	478.00	18.3846		
Nature of family						
Joint family	28	16.6%	485.00	17.3214	**Z-Value**	.304
Nuclear family	141	83.4%	2493.00	17.6809	-1.030	
No. of family members						
Upto 3	25	14.8%	431.00	17.2400	.748	.475
4-6	131	77.5%	2317.00	17.6870		
above 6	13	7.7%	230.00	17.6923		
No. of earning members						
One member	99	58.6%	1758.00	17.7576	6.167	.003**
2 members	59	34.9%	1012.00	17.1525		
above 2	11	6.5%	208.00	18.9091		

Source: Computed data *Significant at 5% level; **Significant at 1% level.

Age

From the table 4.4, it is observed that the mean awareness score of the sample respondents belonging to the category of above 40 years of age is higher than upto 25 years of age, 26 to 40 years of age and the overall mean score. It is proposed to test the following hypothesis by applying F-Test.

H_0: There is no significant relationship between age and awareness level of the sample respondents about Eco-Friendly products.

It is found that the calculated value of F ($p<0.05$) is higher than the theoretical values of F at 1 per cent level of significance. Therefore, the framed hypothesis is rejected. It is concluded that there is a significant relationship between age and awareness level of the sample respondents about Eco-Friendly products.

Gender

The table shows that the mean awareness score of the sample respondents belonging to the category of male is higher than female group and the overall mean score. It is proposed to test the following hypothesis by applying Z-Test.

H_0: There is no significant relationship between gender and awareness level of the sample respondents about Eco-Friendly products.

It is found that the calculated value of Z ($p>0.05$) is less than the theoretical values of Z at 5 per cent level of significance. Therefore, the framed hypothesis is accepted. It is concluded that there is no significant relationship between gender and awareness level of the sample respondents about Eco-Friendly products.

Marital Status

The table depicts that the mean awareness score of the sample respondents belonging to the category of married is higher than unmarried group and the overall mean score. It is proposed to test the following hypothesis by applying Z-Test

H_0: There is no significant relationship between marital status and awareness level of the sample respondents about Eco-Friendly products.

It is found that the calculated value of Z ($p<0.05$) is higher than the theoretical values of Z at 5 per cent level of significance. Therefore, the framed hypothesis is rejected. It is concluded that there is a significant relationship between marital status and awareness level of the sample respondents about Eco-Friendly products.

Education

The table indicates that the mean awareness score of the sample respondents belonging to the category of PG group of education is higher than Up to school, UG, Profession and the overall mean score. It is proposed to test the following hypothesis by applying F-Test.

H_0: There is no significant relationship between education and awareness level of the sample respondents about Eco-Friendly products.

It is found that the calculated value of F ($p<0.01$) is higher than the theoretical values of F at 1 per cent level of significance. Therefore, the framed hypothesis is rejected. It is concluded that there is a significant relationship between education and awareness level of the sample respondents about Eco-Friendly products.

Occupation

The table advocates that the mean awareness score of the sample respondents belonging to the category of others in occupation group is higher than Business/Profession, Private Employee, Govt. employee and the overall mean score. It is proposed to test the following hypothesis by applying F-Test.

H_0: There is no significant relationship between occupation and awareness level of the sample respondents about Eco-Friendly products.

It is found that the calculated value of F ($p<0.01$) is higher than the theoretical values of F at 1 per cent level of significance. Therefore, the framed hypothesis is rejected. It is concluded that there is a significant relationship between occupation and awareness level of the sample respondents about Eco-Friendly products.

Income

The table clearly indicates that the mean awareness score of the sample respondents belonging to the category of above Rs. 25,000 as income is higher than Upto Rs. 10,000, From Rs. 10,001 to Rs. 25,000 and the overall mean score. It is proposed to test the following hypothesis by applying F-Test.

H_0: There is no significant relationship between income and awareness level of the sample respondents about Eco-Friendly products.

It is found that the calculated value of F ($p<0.05$) is higher than the theoretical values of F at 5 per cent level of significance. Therefore, the framed hypothesis is rejected. It is concluded that there is a significant relationship between income and awareness level of the sample respondents about Eco-Friendly products.

Nature of Family

The table depicts that the mean awareness score of the sample respondents belonging to the category of nuclear family is higher than joint family group and the overall mean score. It is proposed to test the following hypothesis by applying Z-Test.

H_0: There is no significant relationship between nature of family and awareness level of the sample respondents about Eco-Friendly products.

It is found that the calculated value of Z ($p>0.05$) is less than the theoretical values of Z at 5 per cent level of significance. Therefore, the framed hypothesis is accepted. It is concluded that there is no significant relationship between nature of family and awareness level of the sample respondents about Eco-Friendly products.

Number of Family Members

The table illustrates that the mean awareness score of the sample respondents belonging to the category of above 6 numbers of family members is higher than 4 to 6 members, up to 3 members and the overall mean score. It is proposed to test the following hypothesis by applying F-Test.

H_0: There is no significant relationship between number of family members and awareness level of the sample respondents about Eco-Friendly products.

It is found that the calculated value of F ($p>0.05$) is less than the theoretical values of F at 5 per cent level of significance. Therefore, the framed hypothesis is accepted. It is concluded that there is no significant relationship between number of family members and awareness level of the sample respondents about Eco-Friendly products.

Number of Earning Members

The table clears that the mean awareness score of the sample respondents belonging to the category of above 2 number of earning members is higher than one member, 2 number of earning members and the overall mean score. It is proposed to test the following hypothesis by applying F-Test.

H_0: There is no significant relationship between number of earning members and awareness level of the sample respondents about Eco-Friendly products.

It is found that the calculated value of F ($p<0.05$) is higher than the theoretical values of F at 1 per cent level of significance. Therefore, the framed hypothesis is rejected. It is concluded that there is a significant relationship between number of earning members and awareness level of the sample respondents about Eco-Friendly products.

The results derived that the age, marital status and income of the respondents on the proposed relationship provides evidence that there is significant relationship with awareness of eco- friendly products. It reveals that education, occupation and number of earning members in the family were highly significant with the awareness of eco- friendly products.

4.4. Determinants Influencing the Consumption of Eco -friendly Product

To understand the influence of determinants on the consumption behaviour towards eco-friendly products, the exploratory factors analysis with KMO and Bartlet's test (Table 4.4) was applied to reduce the factors in order to get the model fit.

Table 4.5: KMO and Bartlett's Test

Kaiser-Meyer-Olkin Measure of Sampling Adequacy.		.859
Bartlett's Test of Sphericity	**Approx. Chi-Square**	5648.236
	Df	378
	Sig	.000

Source: Computed data

The Bartlett's test of sphericity was run along with KMO. Kaiser – Mayer – Olkln measure of sampling adequacy is computed which is found to be .859. It is indicated that the size is good enough for sampling. The overall significance of correlation matrices is tested with Bartlett test of sphericity (chi – square = 5648.236 and significant at .000) support for validity of the factor analysis of the data test.

By gathering information regarding factor analysis, it is understood that the way the factors move, affect the consumers consumption of eco-friendly products. Therefore there are different reasons underlying between consumption of products and satisfaction of eco-friendly products. This will give an opportunity to understand those factors which have more influence in stimulating satisfaction of eco-friendly products through consumption for the purpose 28 statements have been used. The analysis shows the role of selected constructs influencing respondents namely consumption of eco – friendly products (cons), environmental concern (con), satisfaction of eco - friendly products (satis) and awareness eco - friendly products (aw).

Table 4.6: Determinants Influencing on Consumption of Eco -friendly Product

	Component				
	1	2	3	4	Communalities
Cons7	.917				.866
Cons1	.916				.827
Cons8	.914				.827
Cons4	.903				.790
Cons2	.894				.799
Cons5	.892				.686
Cons9	.888				.903
Cons6	.850				.887
Cons3	.848				.809
Con2		.948			.871
Con3		.941			.872
Con5		.932			.835
Con6		.932			.842
Con7		.913			.808
Con4		.898			.722
Con1		.816			.826
Satis1			.890		.798
Satis2			.883		.734
Satis3			.883		.842
Satis7			.872		.838
Satis6			.843		.792
Satis4			.838		.799
Satis5			.827		.786
Aw1				.928	.790
Aw2				.909	.715
Aw3				.907	.705
Aw5				.890	.727
Aw4				.886	.771
Explained variance high each factor	25.791	20.930	18.761	14.756	
Cumulative explained variance	25.791	46.720	65.481	80.237	

Source: Computed data

The results from factor analysis portray the influence of respondents on consumption of eco – friendly products. A certificate of eco-friendly products should ensure that the originality of functional benefits and build itself as a belief of the consumers. So it is clear that the respondents believed eco – friendly products which are having environmental certifications (.917). Respondents compare its price (.916) before buying eco – friendly products because it has rational economics behind the strategy of a product purchase and it denotes product's value. Family is a primary group associated with scare consumption. It may necessitate consuming eco – friendly products by the respondents to protect their family members (.914) from hardship. Culture is a combination of learnt beliefs that directs respondents' behaviour in a specific society. Thus, Culture (.903) affects the respondent's intention to buy eco – friendly products. Availability is also a vital role in transferring the positive aspects of cognitive and affective components into final purchase at the point of consumption. To reflect the current situation, respondents purchase eco – friendly products if they are easily available (.894). Respondents consider performance (.892) of eco – friendly products among those who already use the same products. There are many kinds of risks perceived by consumer. So the respondents consider the declaration of certification regarding environmentally friendly while purchasing a product (.888). A brand value influences the individual's attitude towards products and it has a strong preference towards environment friendly. Thus, the respondents consume branded eco – friendly products (.850). Consumer visits a retail outlet (.848) with an intention of buying an eco–friendly products. If the product is not available the respondents may switch from existing store and decide to buy a product in some other store which has environmentally friendly products. These are the factors which are named as first factor and it was named as consciousness on consumption of eco- friendly products.

The second factor named as environmental concern includes factors which belong to environmentally responsible attributes. The respondents concerned about buying environmentally friendly products (.945), reduce negative environmental impacts of consumption towards environmentally friendly products. Respondents make efforts to buy products that are low in pollutants (.934). Because a number of environmental claims might lead the public to believe that specific environmental problems have been adequately addressed and solved. Usage of eco- friendly bags reduces the use of plastic bags (.931). It brings the society in a social responsible way and it encourages environmentally oriented behaviour among business and their customers. Respondents urge their friends (.926) to buy eco – friendly products because group is the most powerful source to improve the environment friendly behaviour. If the company sells environmentally irresponsible products

(.911), people do not respond to those products while purchasing products. If the respondents understand the potential damage (.896) to the environment, they do not purchase those products. Respondents characterized their self as environmentally responsible (.800).

The third factor is named as satisfaction on the consumption of eco-friendly products. It represents green trust and good health (.878) for using eco-friendly products. In terms of social consequences and endanger the health of the consumer society, consumption has allowed people to become increasingly use eco-friendly products. Consumer satisfaction may provide an idea about how consumers perceive (.872) the benefits of eco-friendly products specific to personal relevant dimensions. It is possible to map the existing products and this enables other similar product to enter the consumer mind. Brand and Packaging (.872) has to satisfy a variety of consumers because packaging protects the product and brand that creates identification of product. While product quality (.860) plays an important role in consuming the products, in which the consumers' satisfaction count can force them to repurchase eco-friendly products. Product involvement (.832) was associated with product satisfaction. Mass Media advertising is the most powerful channel with an ability to reach a large or dispersed market repeatedly and persuasively, which increase hostility towards doubts regarding products. Price (.825) adds to the value of the acquisition in terms of features, which carries a premium to satisfy eco-friendly products to consumers. Eco-Labelling (.815) of a product can communicate a great deal of information which indicates ingredients. It also provides an opportunity to inform the consumer about the environmental performance of the product.

The fourth factor is named as Awareness about eco-friendly products. Well published issues of food poisoning and food additives have made safety issue among consumers. It leads to a growth in eco-friendly products with a perceived safety advantage, such as organic food. It creates awareness regarding the health benefits (.926) of eco-friendly products. Increased awareness about green issues now exists among the population as a whole, as result of increasing consumption of eco-friendly products. Awareness about benefits of eco-friendly products leads purchase due to environmental (.905) damage. Thus, consumers are certainly worried about environment. Point of purchase (.903) displays and signs can increase the odds of capturing consumers' attention, and thereby stimulates purchase and increase the sales. It suggests that consumer purchase decisions are finalized in store. The information is presented in a certifications by numerical and symbols by pictorial form which can be absorbed by consumers during purchase time. Both symbol and certification (.876) rely on eco-friendly purchase for the information that makes them useful. A particular brand might be purchased by a consumer because it helps to simplify the buying process for the consumer and it helps to communicate its competitive advantage. So the respondents need to know the various brands offering eco-friendly products (.874).

From the factor analysis, it has been derived that the high communality value (.903) with observation to consider the declaration of certification regarding environmentally friendly while purchasing a product. Next high communality value (.887) with consumption of branded eco-friendly products and brand value has a strong preference towards environment friendly.

4.5. Relationship of Influencing Determinants towards Eco-friendly Products Consumption among the Respondents – Path Analysis

Path analysis is a statistical technique used primarily to examine the comparative strength of direct and indirect relationship among variables. Path analysis consists of a family of models that depicts the influence of a set of variables on one another. The aim of path analysis is to provide estimate of the magnitude and significance of hypothesized causal connections among sets of variables displayed through the use of path diagram.

In order to identify the factors influencing eco-friendly products consumption among the respondents, a path model has been developed and applied.

Based on the conceptual frame work of the study, in order to identify the variables influencing eco-friendly products consumptions among the respondents, the following hypotheses were framed to test the existence of a linear relationship if any, between the antecedents and intention to buy green products. The following hypotheses were framed and tested.

H1: A significant relationship exists between Awareness of the respondents about eco-friendly productions and consumption of eco-friendly products.

H2: A significant relationship exists between concern about environment and consumption of eco-friendly products.

H3: A significant relationship exists between consumption of eco-friendly products and satisfaction on the consumption of eco-friendly products.

In order to identify the interrelationship factors influencing eco-friendly products consumption, the following hypotheses was framed and tested.

H4: A significant relationship exists between Awareness about eco-friendly products and concern on environment.

The Path analysis was employed to test the two hypotheses (H1 and H3) proposed for direct relationship on the consumption of eco-friendly and next hypothesis (H4) proposed for inter relationship between awareness about eco-friendly products and consumption of eco-friendly products. This analytical technique allows for the evaluation of the overall fit of the proposed model and the estimation of all the corresponding path coefficients simultaneously.

Relationship of Influencing Determinants towards Eco-friendly Products Consumption among the Respondents

In order to identify the relationship between the factors influencing eco-friendly products consumption among the respondents, path analysis was applied. The analysis shows the role of selected constructs influencing respondents consumption on eco-friendly products and satisfaction namely awareness about eco-friendly products (aware), Concern of Environment (Concern), Consumption on eco-friendly products (cosump) and Satisfaction about eco-friendly products (Satis). The result is shown in the figure -----

Relationship of Influencing Factors towards Eco-friendly Products Consumption among the Respondents

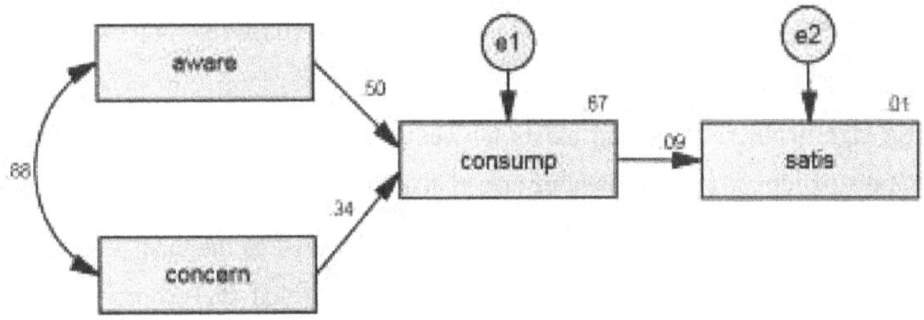

Table 4.7: Goodness of the Fit Statistics for Measurement Model

	Model values	**Suggested values**
CMIN/DF	1.751	≤ 3
RMSEA	0.010	≤ .05
AGFI	0.978	.08
GFI	0.999	.09

Source: Computed data

The obtained result of a chi- square is 3.503, (degrees of freedom 2; P ≤ 0.01). Chi square test is a reasonable measure of fit (Kenny, 2010). CMIN/DF, the relative chi square, is an index of how much the fit of data to model has been reduced by dropping one or more paths. Results of relative chi square is 1.751 (range 1-3), which indicates the best fit (Schumacher and Lomax, 2004).

Goodness of fit index (GFI) 0.996, which is more than 0.9 indicating a best model fit and AGFI 0.978 is also indicating best fit.

Comparative fit indices (CFI) are 0.999, indicating a best fit. It measure as it compares the fit of a target model to the fit of an independent model (a model in which variables are to be uncorrelated). It represents the extent to which the model of interest is better than that of the independent model. Whereas Root Mean Square Error of Approximation (RMSEA) is 0.010 which is best fit since it is less than 0.05.

Table 4.8: Relationship of Factors with Consumption of Eco-friendly Products and Satisfaction

Hypothesis	**Path co-efficient**	**t**
H1: Awareness → Consumption	0.535	5.436**
H2: Concern → Consumption	0.359	3.720**
H3: Consumption → Satisfaction	0.096	1.155

Source: Computed Data ** Significant at 1per cent level

The following are details of hypotheses based on the proven results from figure----through the path analysis.

H1: A significant relationship exists between Knowledge of the respondents about eco-friendly productions and consumption of eco-friendly products.

In this study, Consumption of eco-friendly products is used as the mediating variable for satisfaction about eco-friendly products. The table depicts that the proposed relationship between Awareness of the respondents about eco-friendly productions and consumption of eco-friendly products (H1 → t= 5.436, P < 0.01) is statistically significant.

Suganya D. (2017), suggested that Most of the retailers' concern regarding eco-friendly products are attracted by consumers but because of poor awareness, it has not been fully receive by them. Improving activities on eco-friendly products are the most influential factor that has positively influenced their eco-friendly products awareness (Zillur Rahman Siddique, 2018). Consumers are aware about availability of such products to increase its consumption (Preeti Pillai, 2015).

Hence, the proposed hypothesis H_1 is accepted and there exists the significant relationship between awareness of the respondents about eco-friendly products and consumption of eco-friendly products.

H2: A significant relationship exists between concern about environment and consumption of eco-friendly products.

The results depicts that the relationship exists between concern about environment and consumption of eco-friendly products (H1 → $t= 3.720, P < 0.01$) is statistically significant.

Mainieri, (1997) suggested that a weak relationship exist between environmental concern and pro environmental behaviours. It is sometimes, general attitudes like environmental concern are direct determinants of specific behaviours (Bamberg, 2003). The more environmental concerns have lead to an increase in environmentally friendly purchase behaviors (Manakotla and Jauhari, 2007).

Hence, the proposed hypothesis H_2 is accepted and there exists the significant relationship between concern about environment and consumption of eco-friendly products.

H3: A significant relationship exists between consumption of eco-friendly products and satisfaction on the consumption of eco-friendly products.

In order to test the significant relationship between consumption of eco-friendly products and satisfaction on the consumption of eco-friendly products, satisfaction is used as the dependent variable and consumption is used as the independent variable. The results depicts that the relationship between consumption of eco-friendly products and satisfaction on the consumption of eco-friendly products (H1 → $t= 3.720, P < 0.01$) is statistically significant.

Eco-friendly products positively and significantly influence to Customer satisfaction (Bambang Supriadi, 2017). Consumer satisfaction towards eco - friendly products with the purpose of gaining a deeper understanding on it (Ranjithkumar M.S, 2018) analysis was made. A consumer's purchase behavior depends on the consumer's level of satisfaction towards the product. Purchasing behavior and customer satisfaction is mostly influenced by the attributes of the green products (Ursil Makhdoomi, 2016).

Hence, the proposed hypothesis H_3 is rejected and there is no significant relationship between consumption of eco-friendly products and satisfaction on the consumption of eco-friendly products.

Inter-Relationship of Determinants of Satisfaction on Eco-friendly Products

The study focused on the relationship between determinants and satisfaction on eco-friendly products and investigates the inter relationship between selected constructs which are brought out through the proposed hypothesis (H4).

The table depicts that the interrelationship of variables leads to satisfaction on eco-friendly products.

Table 4.9: Inter-Relationship of factors with Satisfaction on Eco-friendly Products

Hypothesis	Path co-efficient	t
H4: Awareness ↔ Concern	1.737	8.537**

Source: Computed data

H4: A significant relationship exists between Awareness about eco-friendly products and concern on environment.

It is observed from the table (4.9) that the Awareness about eco-friendly products was inter-related to concern on environment. A highly significant inter-relation has been observed (H4 → t= 3.720, P < 0.01). Hence, the proposed all the hypotheses were accepted.

Consumers' environmental concerns do not affect the green products awareness (Zillur Rahman Siddique, (2018). The environmental concerns highly interrelate with eco-friendly products awareness.

Consumers are becoming more aware about environmental issues and this has included knowing about sustainable development. It paved the way for awareness regarding eco-friendly products. (Chen 2008). Perhaps, consumer's environmental concern is related to buying Eco-friendly products and it creates awareness of Eco-friendly products (Zimmer, Stafford, 1994).

Environmental concern was influencing factor that could impact the consumption behaviour of the consumer in a positive way (Boztepe, 2012). It is also supported that awareness has a direct impact on the consumption of Eco-friendly products (Yenoshin and Shinjan, 2005). It was clear that the interrelationship exist between Environmental concern and awareness towards Eco-friendly products. There is not always a positive relation between the consumer concern towards the environment and awareness towards buying behaviour of Eco-friendly products (Hume 1991). Sources of awareness about Eco-friendly products mainly through advertisement which includes ecological and environmental friendly that influence the consumption behaviour of environmental concerned people (Zinkhan and Carlson, 1995).

CHAPTER V

5. Findings, Suggestions and Conclusion

In recent years, many consumers have begun to incorporate environmental concerns in their personal buying decisions through the purchase and use of products. Environmental Concern involves providing consumers with more eco-friendly and socially acceptable products, therefore green consumption must necessitate consuming products in a more sustainable and socially responsible way. The relationship between consumption of eco-friendly products and sustainable development has brought the important association and have inter-connection with environmental concern.

The following findings were derived from the analysis to give the suggestion to marketers.

Socio-economic Profile of the Respondents

- Among the respondents 29.6 per cent belong to the age category of up to 25 years, 39.1 per cent of the respondents belong to 26-50 years and 31.4 per cent of the respondents belong to the age category of above 50 years.
- Of the total sample 29.6 per cent of the respondents belong to the age category of up to 25 years, 39.1 per cent of the respondents belong to 26-50 years and 31.4 per cent of the respondents belong to the age category of above 50 years.
- Majority of the respondents (63.3 per cent) were married and 36.7 per cent of the respondents are unmarried.
- About 49.7 per cent of the respondents belong to the category of up to school level, 39.1 per cent of the respondents are under graduates, 7.1 per cent of the respondents are post graduates and 4.1 per cent of the respondents belong to the category of profession.
- Based on the occupation, 11.2 per cent of the respondents are government employees, 32.0 per cent of the respondents are private employees and 7.7 per cent of the respondents belong to the category of business/profession and the remaining 49.1 per cent of the respondents belong to the occupational category of others.
- With regards to monthly income, 49.7 per cent of the respondents belong to the category of up to Rs.10,000 and 34.9 per cent of the respondents monthly income is from Rs.10,001 to Rs.25,000 and 15.4 per cent of the respondents belong to the category of above Rs.25,000.

- Based on the family type, 16.6 per cent of the respondents belong to joint family and 83.4 per cent of the respondents belong to nuclear family.
- About 14.8 per cent of the respondents belong to the category of up to 3 members, 77.5 per cent of the respondents belong to the category of 4-6 members and 7.7 per cent of the respondents belong to the category of above 6 members.
- On the basis of family size, 58.6 per cent of the respondents belong to the category of 1 member, 34.9 per cent of the respondents belong to the category of 2 members and 6.5 per cent of the respondents belong to the category of above 2 members.

Perception about Eco-friendly Products Purchase

- On the basis of usage towards eco-friendly products, majority (79.88 per cent) of the sample respondents use organic food.
- Majority (38.46 per cent) of the respondents have the motive of concern for the environment to use the eco-friendly products.
- About 38.46 per cent of the respondents have got knowledge about eco-friendly products followed by friendly/relatives (20.12 per cent).
- Place of availability shows, 42.01 per cent of the sample respondents purchase eco-friendly products at local shops, 33.73 per cent purchase at specialize shops/units.
- On the basis of regularity, 34.91 per cent of the sample respondents purchase eco-friendly products once a week, followed by once in a month (30.18 per cent).
- Higher price of Eco-Friendly products was accepted by 71.60 per cent of the sample respondents.
- About 89.35 per cent of the sample respondents consider environment before purchasing eco-friendly products whereas 10.65 per cent of the sample respondents do not consider the environment.
- Majority (95.86 per cent) of the sample respondents change their choice of purchase eco-friendly products when they are seeing eco-labelled whereas 4.14 per cent of the sample respondents do not change their choice.
- About 84.62 per cent of the sample respondents consider that products and packages are designed to be recycled while purchasing products.
- Among 78.70 per cent of the sample respondents trust the quality while purchasing eco-friendly product.
- Majority (94.08 per cent) of the sample respondents are aware of purchasing of eco-friendly product which will contribute to the sustainable development.

- Eco-friendly products are very expensive with a mean score of 51.85 as the main reason for not using eco-friendly products followed by Eco-Friendly products are not available in full range of variety (51.57).
- Certifications (57.08) on eco-friendly product is the main marketing strategy that would influence the purchase behaviour of eco-friendly products.

Awareness Level of Consumers about Eco-Friendly Products based on their Socio-Economic Profile

There is a significant relationship between age, gender, marital status, education, occupation and income of the respondents with awareness of the sample respondents about Eco-Friendly products. There is no significant relationship between nature of family, number of family members, number of earning members and awareness of the sample respondents about Eco-Friendly products.

Determinants Influencing on Consumption of Eco-friendly Product

From the factor analysis, it has been derived that the high communality value (.903) with observation to consider the declaration of certification regarding environmentally friendly while purchasing a product. Next high communality value (.887) with consumption of branded eco-friendly products and brand value has a strong preference towards environment friendly.

The resulted factors were named and their percentage of variance was indicated. The factor includes consumption of eco- friendly products (25.79), environmental concern (20.93), satisfaction on the consumption of eco-friendly products (18.76) and awareness about eco-friendly products.

Relationship of Determinants Influencing Eco-friendly Products Consumption among the Respondents - Path Analysis

In this study, Consumption of eco-friendly products is used as the mediating variable for gauging the satisfaction about eco-friendly products. The table depicts that the proposed relationship between awareness of the respondents about eco-friendly productions and consumption of eco-friendly products (H1 → t = 5.436, P < 0.01) is statistically significant.

The results depicts that the relationship exists between concern about environment and consumption of eco-friendly products (H1 → t = 3.720, P < 0.01) is statistically significant.

In order to test the significant relationship between consumption of eco-friendly products and satisfaction on the consumption of eco-friendly products, satisfaction is used as the dependent variable and consumption is used as the independent variable. The results depicts that the relationship between consumption of eco-friendly products and satisfaction on the consumption of eco-friendly products (H1 → $t = 3.720$, $P < 0.01$) is statistically significant.

It is observed from the table (4.9) that the awareness about eco-friendly products was inter-related to concern on environment. A highly significant inter-relation has been observed (H4 → $t = 3.720$, $P < 0.01$). Hence, all the proposed hypotheses were accepted.

Suggestions

- Customers like best quality of product on any price, so it should add quality for products. Marketer should offer affordable price for product and gifts to be provided with purchasing.
- More emphasis should be given for advertising to create market awareness and to establish a brand image.
- Reviewing awareness of consumers who consume green products in specific geographical regions will immensely help to suppliers, producers, marketers and other relevant parties to stimulate the demand.
- Articulate sustainable consumption policies from government departments are also needed to consumer awareness.
- Environmental awareness should be created in the minds of consumers during their childhood days by providing environmental education at school.
- Eco clubs play an important role in creating environmental awareness amongst the future generation. So eco clubs should be in place in all schools and colleges.
- Consumer knowledge must be expanded for green products by creating effective green marketing campaigns or environmental related activities to the people.
- Consumers are less likely to purchase green products if they are more expensive. So price should be reduced for the eco-friendly products.
- Companies should create advertisement that is more focused on green, eco-friendly image that will influence their customers purchasing decision.

Scope of Future Research

The findings of this study provide various opinions for future research to signify its uses for knowledge and consumption of eco-friendly products. Such in-depth coverage regarding various other factors which has not been mentioned in this study allows to assess dimensions. This enables research to develop an understanding of study the area, the consumer tend to understand relation between consumption of eco- friendly products and their satisfaction of eco - friendly practices. The study utilised quantitative data, and hence it provides detailed description of consumers' consumption and satisfaction towards eco- friendly products. Therefore its findings exhibit an informative framework for further research.

Conclusion

The results of this study focus on the significant and prime-concern of investigating relationship between socio - economic profile and Awareness of eco - friendly products. Majority of the variables regarding socio-economic profile of the respondents were significant and there exist relationship with Awareness of eco-friendly products. It is observed from the analysis Eco-friendly products are very expensive and it was the main reason for not using eco-friendly products, followed by Eco-Friendly products are not available in full range of variety. The results of causal effect reveal evidence that of significant relationship between Awareness and environmental concern towards consumption of eco - friendly products. The findings from analysis indicate the relationship between eco - friendly products and consumer satisfaction does not have significantly influence towards products. It shows that not only the satisfaction simply created by consumption of products but also affect by certification of eco - friendly products and branded eco - friendly products. Analysis of environmental concern and Awareness of eco - friendly products create consumption and those have significant relationship regarding consumption of eco - friendly products. But consumption does not create satisfaction and the relationship between them is insignificant.

References

Journals

[1] Afzaal Ali & Israr Ahmad (2012), "Environment Friendly Products: Factors that Influence the Green Purchase Intentions of Pakistani Consumers", Pak. j. eng. technol. sci. Volume 2(1), pp. no. 84-117.

[2] Annesahmad et al (2015), "Consumers Intentions to Purchase Green Brands: The Role of Environmental Concern, Environmental Knowledge and Self-Expressive Benefits", Department of Management Studies, Indian School of Mines, 10(3), pp no. 879-889.

[3] Anu Varghese et al (2015), "A Study on Consumer Perception on Eco - Friendly Products with Reference to Kollam District in Kerala", EPRA International Journal of Economic and Business Review, v 3(7), pp no. 146 -148.

[4] Arcury, T.A. (1990). Environmental attitude and environmental knowledge. Human Organization.

[5] Asha P. et al., (2017) "Consumer Awareness towards Green Products", International Journal of Management (IJM), 8(5), pp no. 8-14.

[6] Bambang Supriadi et al., (2017) "Green Product and Its Impact on Customer Satisfaction", IOSR Journal of Business and Management (IOSR-JBM), 19(8), 35-42.

[7] Birgelen, M., Semeijn, J., & Keicher, M. (2008). "Packaging and Pro environmental Consumption Behavior".

[8] Boztepe (2012), "Green Marketing and Its Impact on Consumer Buying Behavior", European journal of economic and political studies.

[9] Chang, C. (2011). "Feeling Ambivalent about Going Green - Implication for Green Advertising Processing", Journal of Advertising, 40(4), 9-319.

[10] Christopher Gan et al., (2008). "Consumer Purchasing Behavior towards Green Products in New Zeeland", Innovative Marketing, 4(1) pp. no. 93 - 102.

[11] Dunlap, R., and Jones, R. (2002). "Environmental concern: Conceptual and measurement issues", In Handbook of environmental sociology, ed. Greenwood.

[12] Genesis Guanghai MA (2018). "The Effects of Environmental Awareness and Consumption Value on Green Make Up Product Purchase Intentions", Scientific Research Publishing, pp no. 1898 - 1916.

[13] Glegg, G., Richards, J., Heard, J., & Dawson, J. (2005). "Barriers to Green Buying: Household Chemicals", Journal of Sustainable Development, 11(3).

[14] Grace K. Dagher et al., (2015). "Impact of Environmental Concern and Attitude on Green Purchasing Behavior: Gender as the Moderates", Contemporary Management Research, v 11(2) pp. no. 179 - 206.

[15] Kamonthip Maichum (2017). "The Influence of Environmental Concern and Environmental Attitude on Purchase Intention towards Green Products: A Case Study of Young Consumers in Thailand", International Journal of Business Marketing and Management (IJBMM) Volume 2 (3), pp. 01-08.

[16] Khealo P.P et al (2014). "Environmental Concern, Attitude towards Green Products and Green Purchase Intentions of Consumers in Lesotho", Ethiopean Journal of Environmental Studies and Management, 7(4), 361 - 370.

[17] Madu, B.C. and Akob, Thomas Ogbeche (2014). "A Path Analysis of Parental Socio-Economic Status and Home Education Environment on Students' Academic Achievement in the Secondary Schools in Benue State, Nigeria", International Journal of Humanities and Social Science, Vol. 4, No. 10(1), pp no. 117

[18] Magali Morel et al., (2012). "Green marketing: Consumers' Attitudes towards Eco-friendly Products and Purchase Intention in the Fast Moving Consumer Goods (FMCG) sector", pp no. 1- 107.

[19] Maheswari et al., (2014). "Customer's attitude and awareness towards green products with reference to Coimbatore - An analytical study", International Journal of Multidisciplinary Research and Development, v 2(1), pp no. 152-158

[20] Meenakshi Saratha M. (2015). "A Study on Customer Satisfaction Level on Green Products with Special Reference to Coimbatore District", International Journal of Multidisciplinary Research and Development v 2 (3), pp no. 292-295.

[21] Mohd Danish Kiramani et al., (2016). "Environmental Concern and Attitude towards Green Products: Evidence from India", Serbian Journal of Management, 11(2), 159–179.

[22] Naazahmohdsuki (2013). "Green Awareness Effects on Consumers Purchasing Decision: Some Insights from Malaysia", IJAPS v 9 (2), pp no. 23 -37.

[23] Nandini Desai (2015). "A Study of Consumer Awareness: Towards Eco Friendly Buildings in Pune City", international journal of business quantitative economics and applied management research, v 1(8), pp no. 15-23.

[24] Nargesdelafrooz et al., (2014). "Effects of Green Marketing on Consumer Purchase Behavior", Foundation Journal, pp no. 2-9.

[25] Nufazil Altaf (2013). "Consumers Awareness towards Green Marketing - A Study of Srinagar City", Asian Journal of Managerial Science, 2(2), pp. no, 37-43.

[26] Parthiban V.N. (2016), "Consumer Perception towards the Green Marketing: A Study with Special Reference to Chennai City", Int. Journal of Management and Development Studies 5(4), 52 -60.

[27] Preeti Pillai et al., (2015). "A Study on Consumers' Perception towards Eco-friendly Products in Ahmedabad", International Journal of Research in IT and Management, 6(7), 14-28.

[28] Preeti Sehgal (2010)," Impact of Eco-Friendly Products on Consumer, Behavior", CBS E-Journal, Biz n Bytes, Vol. 6, pp no. 121- 146.

[29] R. Rajasekaran et al., (2013). "A Study on Green Product and Innovation for Sustainable Development", Global Journal of Management and Business Studies, 3(6), 625-632.

[30] Ranjithkumar M.S et al., (2018). "A Study on Consumers Level of Satisfaction towards Eco-Friendly Products", IJRAR- International Journal of Research and Analytical Reviews, volume 5(4), pp no. 425 - 427.

[31] Roberts, J.A. (1996), "Green consumers in the 1990s: profile and implications for advertising", Journal of Business Research.

[32] Saira Yasin Lasbela, U.J. (2015). "Green Marketing: A Study of Consumers' Attitude towards Environment Friendly Products", Sci. Techl., v 6, pp. 109-116.

[33] Sanjeevkumar et al., (2012). "Consumer Awareness and Perception towards Green Product: A Study of Youngsters in India", International Journal of Marketing and Business Communication, 1(4), 36-47.

[34] Schahn, J., & Holzer, E. (1990). "Studies of individual environmental concern. Environment and Behavior."

[35] Shirmila Stanley (2015). "The Perception and Impact of Sustainable Green Consumption Practices and Women in Preserving Ecology with Special Reference to Chennai City", Journal of Economics, Business and Management, 3(10), 917 -923.

[36] Soegoto D.S (2018). "Analysis of Eco - Friendly Preference and Eco - Friendly Product Quality; Their Implications to Customer Satisfaction", IOP Conf. Series: Materials Science and Engineering, pp no. 1-7.

[37] Sudhirachdev (2011). "Eco - Friendly Products and Consumer Perception", International Journal of Multidisciplinary Research, v 1 (5), pp no. 279 - 287.

[38] Suganya D. (2017), "A Study on Consumer Awareness towards Eco-Friendly Products at Coimbatore", International Journal of Current Research and Modern Education (IJCRME), 2(1), pp. no. 237 241.

[39] Suresh Kumar D. (2015) "A Study of Consumers' Perception and Attitude towards Green Products", International Journal of Advanced Research in Management and Social Sciences, 4(8), pp. no. 285 - 297.

[40] Tan Booi Chen et al., (2010). "Attitude towards the Environment and Green Products: Consumers' Perspective", Management Science and Engineering, Vol. 4 (2), pp. 27-39.

[41] Triantafillidou, A., & Siomkos, G. (2014). "Consumption experience outcomes: satisfaction, nostalgia intensity, word-of-mouth communication and behavioural intentions", Journal of Consumer Marketing, vol. 31(6/7), 526-540.

[42] Wiwik Handayani (2017) conducted a study on "Green Consumerism: An Eco-Friendly Behaviour form through the Green Product Consumption and Green Marketing", SINERGI, Volume 7(2), pp no. 25-29.

[43] Yatish Joshi and Zillur Rahman (2015), "Factors Affecting Green Purchase Behaviour and Future Research, International Strategic Management Review 3 (2015) 128–14

[44] Zainabzurfiquar (2015), "Green Marketing: Environmental Concern and Customer Satisfaction", European Journal of Business and Management, 7(1), pp no. 115- 126.

[45] Zillur Rahman Siddique et al., (2018) "Sources of Consumers Awareness toward Green Products and Its Impact on Purchasing Decision in Bangladesh", Journal of Sustainable Development; Vol. 11(3), pp. no. 9 -22.

[46] Zimmer & Stafford (1994), "Green Issues: Dimensions of Environmental Concern", Journal of business research, vol 30(1), pp no. 63-74.

[47] Zinkhan and Carlson (1995), "Green advertising and the reluctant consumer", journal of advertising, vol (2), 1-6.

Books

[48] Abdul Kalam A.P.J & Srijan Pal Singh (2011). "Target 3 Billion - Innovation Solutions towards Sustainable Development", Penguin Books, New Delhi.

[49] Aparna P. & Goyal (2018). "Environment - Friendly Products - Adapt Green now", Partridge India.

[50] Geoffrey P. Lantos. (2011). "Consumer Behaviour in Action - Real life applications for marketing managers", Yes Dee Publishing Pvt. Ltd.

[51] Gopal Bhargava (2003). Environmental Challenges and Sustainable Future, Kalpaz Publications, Delhi.

[52] Joy D. Lindquist & Joseph Sirgy M (2009). "Consumer Behaviour", Cengage Learning India, New Delhi.

[53] Kenpeattie (1995). Environmental Marketing Management - meeting the green Challenge, Pitman Publishing, London.

[54] Kotler P and Keller 2009 Marketing Management. 13th ed. (New Jersey: Pearson Pretince Hall) pp. 123, 164, 516.

[55] Leon G. Schiffman, Joseph Wiseblit and Ramesh Kumar S. (2017). "Consumer Behaviour", Pearson India Education Services Pvt. Ltd., India.

[56] Lucie Middlemiss (2016). "Sustainable Consumption - Key issues in environment and sustainability".

[57] Michael R. Solomon (2017). "Consumer Behaviour - Buying, Having and Being", Indian Subcontinent Adaption, Pearson India Education Services Pvt. Ltd., India.

[58] Monica Loss (2013). Green Marketing - Marketing Strategies and Consumer Behaviour, New Delhi, India, Global Vision Publishing House.

[59] Ottman, J.A. (1993). "Green Marketing: Opportunity for Innovation". McGraw Hill, NT Business Books, Chicago.

[60] Paul peter .J and Jerry C. Olson (2002). Consumer Behaviour and Marketing Strategy, McGraw-Hill, New York.

[61] Peattie, K. (1992). Green Marketing, London, Pitman Publishing.

[62] Ramakrishnan P.S. (2013). Ecology and Sustainable Development - Working with Knowledge System, National Book Trust, India.

[63] Ramanuj Majumdar (2010). "Consumer Behaviour- insights from Indian market", PHI Learning Pvt. Ltd.

[64] Ramesh Kumar S. (2013). Case studies in Consumer Behaviour, Dorling Kindersley India.

[65] Ramesh Kumar S. (2017). Consumer Behaviour - The Indian Context (Concepts and Cases), Pearson India Education Services Pvt. Ltd., India.

[66] Robert Dahlstrom (2011). "Green Marketing Theory, Practice and Strategies", New Delhi, Cengage Learning India Private limited.

[67] Robert East, Malcolm Wright & Marc Vanhuele (2009), "Consumer Behaviour - Applications in Marketing", Sage Publications India Pvt. Ltd., New Delhi.

[68] Roger D. Blackwell, Paul W. Miniard, James F. Engel & Zilllur Rahman (2006). Cengage Learning India, New Delhi.

[69] Sakarama Somayaji & Ganesh Somayaji (2009). "Environmental Concerns and Sustainable Development - Some Perspectives from India", Teri publishing books, New Delhi.

[70] SrabantI Mukherjee (2012). "Consumer Behaviour", Cengage Learning India, New Delhi.

[71] TV Rao (1996). "Human Resources Development - Experiences Interventions Strategies", Sage Publications India Pvt. Ltd., New Delhi.

[72] Verma P.K (2012). "Greeen Marketing Issues and Challenges", Mumbai, Yiking Books, Jaipur.